POEMS (

ARTHUR O'SHA

SELECTED AND EDITED BY
WILLIAM ALEXANDER PERCY

British Library Cataloguing-in-Publication Data
A catalogue record for this book is available from the
British Library

William Alexander Percy

William Alexander Percy was born on 14 May, 1885 in Greenville, Mississippi, USA. His mother, Camille, was a strong French Catholic, and his father, LeRoy Percy was the last United States Senator from Mississippi, elected by legislature. The family were very influential in the state, owning 20,000 acres of cotton plantation, and Percy used this influence to champion his mother's Catholic religion in an overwhelmingly Protestant area. As a young man, Percy travelled to Paris before reading law at *Harvard University*. He joined his father's law firm after graduating. During the First World War, Percy served in Belgium as a delegate to the *Commission for Relief in Belgium*, and remained there until America declared war in 1917. Thereafter, Percy served in the US army, earning the rank of Captain and was awarded the *Croix de Guerre* for his bravery. On returning from the war, Percy edited the *Yale Younger Poets* series (until 1932) and also published four further volumes of poetry with the *Yale University Press*. It was here that he befriended many members of the contemporary literary elite as well as several members of the *Harlem Renaissance*, a movement which promoted African-American cultural expression. Having known Herbert Hoover from his time in the *Belgium Relief Effort*, Percy was placed in charge of relief during the great flood of 1927. He was incredibly concerned about the poor conditions, healthcare and nutrition offered to the mainly black refugees fleeing flooded farms and plantations across Mississippi. Percy believed that the people needed to be evacuated to nearby Vicksburg in Warren County to ensure their health and wellbeing. However after several local planters, including Percy's own father, opposed the decision, conditions for the refugees deteriorated severely and Percy was strongly criticised in the national press. After this debacle, he soon resigned. Percy is best known for his memoir, *Lanterns on the Levee: Recollections of a Planter's Son,* published in 1941, but he also wrote poetry, published in *Collected Poems* (1943) and the text of *They Cast Their Nets in Galilee,* included in the *Episcopal Hymnal* (1982). He died on 21 January, 1954, at the age of 69.

Table of Contents.

v

TABLE OF CONTENTS

Introduction.

ONCE, a long time ago, when American poetry meant Longfellow and Poe and Lowell (the elder), or at the latest Lanier, and when a first reading of the great and latterly despised Victorians was an enchantment, a gust of delight, another young haunter of the purlieus of Parnassus and myself discovered a poem which began:

> We are the music makers
> And we are the dreamers of dreams.

(The week before, our find had been Matthew Arnold's "Dover Beach": mostly those were red-letter days.) The author's name was new to us. It was Arthur W. E. O'Shaughnessy. Then, as the precious volume through which we were browsing happened to be Palgrave's *Golden Treasury,* we hastened to take to our hearts "The Fountain of Tears," "John the Baptist," and "Song of Palms." From that hour Arthur O'Shaughnessy was, for us, of the immortals.

Our enthusiasm started us on a search for anything and everything by him or about him — efforts almost entirely unrewarded. Even Ward's *English Poets* — that amber for riflers of the honeyed heights — added but one page to our scanty store of information, though that one was from the usually judicious and always charming pen of Mr. Edmund Gosse. He summarized for us aptly and justly O'Shaughnessy's genius, named what he considered his five best pieces (three of which are in my judgment among his least successful attempts), and observed that his poetic vein was thin and soon exhausted, his earliest volume having most of it and his last none of it. Years afterwards I found that last volume and read it with a doubt that Mr. Gosse had done as much, for it contains such typical and lovely examples of the very vein praised by him as "Silences," "If She But Knew," and

1

"A Love Symphony." Intermittently I continued my search with indifferent success, the Congressional Library yielding "An Epic of Women," and the New York Public Library, "Lays of France." The fact was, his four volumes, "An Epic of Women" (1870), "Lays of France" (1872), "Music and Moonlight" (1874), and "Songs of a Worker" (posthumously published, 1881), were out of print, nor have they since been reprinted or issued as a collection, and, stranger still, no selection from them has been published either in England or America, with the exception of the slim and exquisite group printed by Mr. Mosher in one of the Bibelots, and the somewhat lengthier group appended by Louise Chandler Moulton to her sketch of O'Shaughnessy's life and work and issued in a lovely format by Stone and Kimball nearly thirty years ago.

Such being the situation, the Yale University Press, thinking perhaps, with me, that even the most beautiful things perish if the opportunity for reading or seeing or hearing them is not offered the vexed and hurrying children of men, has undertaken here the pious task of making O'Shaughnessy's finest poems accessible to readers of English poetry. It has not been thought advisable to attempt the publication of his complete works, because they are by no means of uniform excellence. But his best is unique, of a haunting beauty, a very precious heritage.

Much could be written, I suppose, of the influences discernible or easily imagined in O'Shaughnessy's art; of his rhymes and rhythm like Swinburne's, of his spiritual affinity to Poe, of his choice of words and themes suggesting Rossetti, of recurring hints of the French poets he loved. But after all, such discussions are neither very interesting nor very fruitful. Besides, when O'Shaughnessy wrote something that was worth reading at all, he wrote something utterly different from anything that had been written before—or since, for that matter. His quality is, above all, individual. Here is a poet who had no range, no profundity or originality of thought, no interest, so far as his art reveals, in everyday life, or simple joys and sorrows, or heroic deeds, no ability to construct or invent a tale because facts in themselves meant nothing to him. Yet here is a poet, authentically of the sacred band, blessed with the divine gusto. This he is because of the gift of music and the gift of ecstasy. The latter not infrequently failed him, leaving his verse with only a swooning sweetness, flat and flavorless. But when the ecstasy was upon him he had, as Palgrave put it, "the exquisite tenderness of touch, the melody and delicacy" of his favorite composer, Chopin. He is a singer or nothing. And he sang as a singer should — with intoxication, with happy madness, happy even when the subject of his song is heartbreak or hopeless grief. The things of which he sang, over and over again as a bird sings, were love, death, and that visionary land of escape that all singers for their solace conjure up, for him a land of palms washed with infinitudes of light. Yet the love and the death and the far land of his song are not those we know or have even dreamed of. They are peculiarly his own. He sings of them with such simplicity and directness and naïveté that one might suppose they had never been sung of before. With a like ingenuous freshness Giotto must have painted, and some spring-voiced French poet have written of Aucassin and Nicolette. Unmoral he surely is, what the world calls sin presenting itself to him as a personal antagonism, not understood but resented. All that is wistful and hopeless and baleful in love he seems to have experienced. Perhaps the Freudians would say he suffered from an unsatisfied sex complex. My care, however, is to give thanks for hearing his rapturous outcry, no matter what the pain or the delight from which it sprang. His very words and cadences seem rimmed with rapture, piercing and strange, unearthly and very clear. If I were passing the Siren Isles, one of the songs I know I should hear drifting across the waves would be that which Sarrazine sang to her dead lover in "Chaitivel":

> Hath any loved you well, down there,
> Summer or winter through?

3

> Down there, have you found any fair
> Laid in the grave with you?
> Is death's long kiss a richer kiss
> Than mine was wont to be—
> Or have you gone to some far bliss
> And quite forgotten me?

A hackneyed stanza form, no single unusual or colorful word, indeed an almost complete series of monosyllables, no tangible thought, yet magic—and magic continued for seven stanzas!

He was not always so happy in sustaining the flight of his song. The three perfect opening stanzas of the "Ode" are succeeded by four so inferior as to be commonplace. Palgrave calmly omitted them and I have followed his example, not only with the "Ode" itself, but with possibly one-fourth of the poems here given. I confess I look with horror at an editor arrogating to himself such omniscience; but in O'Shaughnessy's case it is the only way to save him from himself and for posterity. I am certain, understanding my motive, he would pardon my presumption along with any errors of judgment.

It was probably his skill in the technique of versification that tempted him so often to repetition, to keeping on after he had said what he had to say. So perfect was his ear he was never unmusical even when he was saying nothing. His marvellous sense of the value of vowels and consonants, his flair for rhyme, the rise and fall of his own cadences, intoxicated him into diffuseness and lured him into using certain words again and again just because the sound of them was to him beautiful. Though surely a conscious artist, he lacked the ability to criticise his own work. Probably he gauged it only by the vividness or sincerity of the emotion he was attempting to trap in words. "The Daughter of Herodias," in spite of many stanzas haunting in sound and color, is structurally appalling. Nor is there any impression of architecture, of building, in the "Lays" with the exception of "Chaitivel." That sweetness long drawn out succeeded, I am sure, because it is mood, ecstasy, and not narrative, through its whole length. The events of the story which might well have been dramatically presented are slurred, indeed hardly told, but the feelings, at once eerie and poignant, of Sarrazine and her lovers are luxuriously detailed and the enchanted descriptions are vague and vivid as a dream. And too, Sarrazine's love, unwillingly cruel and unfaithful, dreamy and yearning, is the love over which O'Shaughnessy seems to have brooded long and often, a lyrical theme of which he never wearied.

"Bisclavaret," usually regarded as standing apart from the rest of his work, baffles analysis, but the underlying idea of it seems to me to be the very background of O'Shaughnessy's emotional life, seen here only in glimpses and under the guise of fantasy. Though a ballad in form, it tells no story, and though half of its stanzas are descriptions of scenery, descriptions singularly strange and accurate and unreal, the impulse to write it arose, I am certain, not from a wish to describe storms and moonlight and desolate wastes, but from an emotion bitterly real and personal to the poet. What that emotion is, I am not sure. My guess would be he is still singing of love, not an individualized love this time, but of that spring storm within a man, vehement and undirected and lawless, which we usually term sex. Whatever it means, the poem is well-nigh perfect and without counterpart in English verse.

Will those who love this man's poetry require that this brief introduction tell something of the facts of his life? If I say that London was the place of his birth and death, the year of the former being 1844, of the latter 1881, that he was employed as an ichthyologist in the British Museum, that his high spirits and personal charm made him a welcome member of the Ford Madox Brown-Rossetti circle, that he married the daughter of Dr. Westland Marston in 1873 and within six years had lost both her and his two children, I shall have said all that the occasion demands, though doubtless I shall have satisfied no one. If further I am pressed to explain what were those inward facts of his life that so evidently colored his art, I shall have to answer I do not know. But if I did, let me add, I should not tell. By some sorcery this man produced beauty of a rare and charmed and perfect kind, and this he gave the world. For this let the lovers of beauty offer thanks to the high gods unquestioningly, remembering that many men have lived their lives and loved their loves, good or ill, blissful or wretched, without learning his enchanted speech.

WILLIAM ALEXANDER PERCY.

FROM
"AN EPIC OF WOMEN"

Exile.

Des voluptés intérieures
Le sourire mystérieux.

VICTOR HUGO

A common folk I walk among;
I speak dull things in their own tongue:
   But all the while within I hear
   A song I do not sing for fear—
How sweet, how different a thing!
   And when I come where none are near
I open all my heart and sing.

I am made one with these indeed,
And give them all the love they need—
   Such love as they would have of me:
   But in my heart—ah, let it be!—
I think of it when none is nigh.
   There is a love they shall not see;
For it I live, for it will die.

And oft-times, though I share their joys,
And seem to praise them with my voice,
   Do I not celebrate my own,
   Ay, down in some far inward zone
Of thoughts in which they have no part?
   Do I not feel—ah, quite alone
With all the secret of my heart?

O when the shroud of night is spread
On these, as Death is on the dead,
   So that no sight of them shall mar
   The blessed rapture of a star—
Then I draw forth those thoughts at will;
   And like the stars those bright thoughts are;
And boundless seems the heart they fill:

9

For every one is as a link;
And I enchain them as I think;
　　Till present and remembered bliss,
　　And better, worlds on after this,
I have—led on from each to each
　　Athwart the limitless abyss—
In some surpassing sphere I reach.

I draw a veil across my face
Before I come back to the place
　　And dull obscurity of these;
　　I hide my face, and no man sees;
I learn to smile a lighter smile,
　　And change, and look just what they please.
It is but for a little while.

I go with them; and in their sight
I would not scorn their little light,
　　Nor mock the things they hold divine;
　　But when I kneel before the shrine
Of some base deity of theirs,
　　I pray all inwardly to mine,
And send my soul up with my prayers:

For I—ah, to myself I say—
I have a heaven though far away;
　　And there my Love went long ago,
　　With all the things my heart loves so;
And there my songs fly, every one:
　　And I shall find them there, I know,
When this sad pilgrimage is done.

The Fair Maid and the Sun.

O sons of men, that toil, and love with tears!

Know ye, O sons of men, the maid who dwells
Between the two seas at the Dardanelles?

10

Her face hath charmed away the change of years,
And all the world is fillèd with her spells.

No task is hers for ever, but the play
Of setting forth her beauty day by day:
　　There in your midst, O sons of men that toil,
She laughs the long eternity away.

The chains about her neck are many-pearled,
Rare gems are those round which her hair is curled;
　　She hath all flesh for captive, and for spoil,
The fruit of all the labour of the world.

She getteth up and maketh herself bare,
And letteth down the wonder of her hair
　　Before the sun; the heavy golden locks
Fall in the hollow of her shoulders fair.

She taketh from the lands, as she may please,
All jewels, and all corals from the seas;
　　She layeth them in rows upon the rocks;
Laugheth, and bringeth fairer ones than these.

Five are the goodly necklaces that deck
The place between her bosom and her neck;
　　She passeth many a bracelet o'er her hands;
And, seeing she is white without a fleck,

And, seeing she is fairer than the tide,
And of a beauty no man can abide —
　　Proudly she standeth as a goddess stands,
And mocketh at the sun and sea for pride:

And to the sea she saith: "O silver sea,
Fair art thou, but thou art not fair like me;
　　Open thy white-toothed dimpled mouths and try;
They laugh not the soft way I laugh at thee."

And to the sun she saith: "O golden sun,
Fierce is thy burning till the day is done;

11

But thou shalt burn mere grass and leaves, while I
Shall burn the hearts of men up every one."

O fair and dreadful is the maid who dwells.
Between the two seas at the Dardanelles:
  As fair and dread as in the ancient years;
And still the world is fillèd with her spells,

O sons of men, that toil, and love with tears!

The Cypress.

O Ivory bird, that shakest thy wan plumes,
  And dost forget the sweetness of thy throat
  For a most strange and melancholy note—
That wilt forsake the summer and the blooms
  And go to winter in a place remote!

The country where thou goest, Ivory bird!
  It hath no pleasant nesting-place for thee;
  There are no skies nor flowers fair to see,
Nor any shade at noon—as I have heard—
  But the black shadow of the Cypress tree.

The Cypress tree, it groweth on a mound;
  And sickly are the flowers it hath of May,
  Full of a false and subtle spell are they;
For whoso breathes the scent of them around,
  He shall not see the happy Summer day.

In June, it bringeth forth, O Ivory bird!
  A winter berry, bitter as the sea;
  And whoso eateth of it, woe is he—
He shall fall pale, and sleep—as I have heard—
  Long in the shadow of the Cypress tree.

A Whisper from the Grave.

MY life points with a radiant hand,
  Along a golden ray of sun
That lights some distant promised land,
  A fair way for my feet to run:
My Death stands heavily in gloom,
And digs a soft bed in the tomb
  Where I may sleep when all is done.

The flowers take hold upon my feet;
  Fair fingers beckon me along;
I find Life's promises so sweet
  Each thought within me turns to song:
But Death stands digging for me — lest
Some day I need a little rest,
  And come to think the way too long.

O seems there not beneath each rose
  A face? — the blush comes burning through;
And eyes my heart already knows
  Are filling themselves from the blue,
Above the world; and One, whose hair
Holds all my sun, is coming, fair,
  And must bring heaven if all be true:

And now I have face, hair, and eyes;
  And lo, the Woman that these make
Is more than flower, and sun, and skies!
  Her slender fingers seem to take
My whole fair life, as 'twere a bowl,
Wherein she pours me forth her soul,
  And bids me drink it for her sake.

Methinks the world becomes an isle;
  And there — immortal, as it seems —
I gaze upon her face, whose smile
  Flows round the world in golden streams:

13

Ah, Death is digging for me deep,
Lest some day I should need to sleep
   And solace me with other dreams!

But now I feel as though a kiss
   Of hers should ever give me birth
In some new heaven of life-long bliss;
   And heedlessly, athwart my mirth,
I see Death digging day by day
A grave; and, very far away,
   I hear the falling of the earth.

Ho there, if thou wilt wait for me,
   Thou Death!—I say—keep in thy shade;
Crouch down behind the willow tree,
   Lest thou shouldst make my love afraid;
If thou hast aught with me, pale friend,
Some flitting leaf its sigh shall lend
   To tell me when the grave is made!

And lo, e'en while I now rejoice,
   Encircled by my love's fair arm,
There cometh up to me a voice,
   Yea, through the fragrance and the charm;
Quite like some sigh the forest heaves
Quite soft—a murmur of dead leaves,
   And not a voice that bodeth harm:

O lover, fear not—have thou joy;
   For life and love are in thy hands:
I seek in no wise to destroy
   The peace thou hast, nor make the sands
Run quicker through thy pleasant span;
Blest art thou above many a man,
   And fair is She who with thee stands:

I only keep for thee out here—
   O far away, as thou hast said,
Among the willow trees—a clear

14

Soft space for slumber, and a bed;
That after all, if life be vain,
And love turn at the last to pain,
    Thou mayst have ease when thou art dead.

O grieve not: back to thy love's lips,
    Let her embrace thee more and more,
Consume that sweet of hers in sips:
    I only wait till it is o'er;
For fear thou'lt weary of her kiss,
And come to need a bed like this
    Where none shall kiss thee evermore.

Believe each pleasant muttered vow
    She makes to thee, and see with ease
Each promised heaven before thee now;
    I only think, if one of these
Should fail thee — O thou wouldst need then
To come away right far from men,
    And weep beneath the willow trees.

And, therefore, have I made this place,
    Where thou shouldst come on that hard day,
Full of a sad and weary grace;
    For here the drear wind hath its way
With grass, and flowers, and withered tree —
As sorrow shall that day with thee,
    If it should happen as I say.

And, therefore, have I kept the ground,
    As 'twere quite holy, year by year;
The great wind lowers to a sound
    Of sighing as it passes near;
And seldom doth a man intrude
Upon the hallowed solitude,
    And never but to shed a tear.

So, if it be thou come, alas,
    For sake of sorrow long and deep,

I — Death, the flowers, and leaves, and grass —
  Thy grief-fellows, do mourn and weep:
Or if thou come, with life's whole need
To rest a life-long space indeed,
  I too and they do guard thy sleep.

Moreover, sometimes, while all we
  Have kept the grave with heaviness,
The weary place hath seemed to be
  Not barren of all blessedness:
Spent sunbeams rest them here at noon,
And grieving spirits from the moon
  Walk here at night in shining dress.

And there is gazing down on all
  Some great and love-like eye of blue,
Wherefrom, at times, there seem to fall
  Strange looks that soothe the place quite through;
As though indeed, if all love's sweet
And all life's good should prove a cheat,
  They knew some heaven that might be true.

— It is a tender voice like this
  That comes to me in accents fair:
Well; and through much of love and bliss,
  It seemeth not a thing quite bare
Of comfort, e'en to be possest
Of that one spot of earth for rest,
  Among the willow trees down there.

Bisclavaret.

Bisclaveret ad nun en Bretan,
Garwall l'apelent li Norman.
Jadis le poët-hum oïr,
E souvent suleit avenir,
Humes plusurs Garwall devindrent
E es boscages meisun tindrent.

MARIE DE FRANCE: LAIS

In *either mood, to bless or curse,*
God bringeth forth the breath of man;
No angel sire, no woman nurse
Shall change the work that God began:

One spirit shall be like a star,
He shall delight to honour one;
Another spirit he shall mar:
None shall undo what God hath done.

The weaker holier season wanes;
Night comes with darkness and with sins;
And, in all forests, hills, and plains,
A keener, fiercer life begins.

And, sitting by the low hearth fires,
I start and shiver fearfully;
For thoughts all strange and new desires
Of distant things take hold on me;

And many a feint of touch or sound
Assails me, and my senses leap
As in pursuit of false things found
And lost in some dim path of sleep.

But, momently, there seems restored
A triple strength of life and pain;
I thrill, as though a wine were poured
Upon the pore of every vein:

I burn — as though keen wine were shed
  On all the sunken flames of sense —
Yea, till the red flame grows more red,
  And all the burning more intense,

And, sloughing weaker lives grown wan
  With needs of sleep and weariness,
I quit the hallowed haunts of man
  And seek the mighty wilderness.

—Now over intervening waste
  Of lowland drear, and barren wold,
I scour, and ne'er assuage my haste,
  Inflamed with yearnings manifold;

Drinking a distant sound that seems
  To come around me like a flood;
While all the track of moonlight gleams
  Before me like a streak of blood;

And bitter stifling scents are past
  A-dying on the night behind,
And sudden piercing stings are cast
  Against me in the tainted wind.

And lo, afar, the gradual stir,
  And rising of the stray wild leaves;
The swaying pine, and shivering fir,
  And windy sound that moans and heaves

In first fits, till with utter throes
  The whole wild forest lolls about:
And all the fiercer clamour grows,
  And all the moan becomes a shout;

And mountains near and mountains far
  Breathe freely: and the mingled roar
Is as of floods beneath some star
  Of storms, when shore cries unto shore.

But soon, from every hidden lair
  Beyond the forest tracts, in thick

Wild coverts, or in deserts bare,
  Behold They come — renewed and quick —

The splendid fearful herds that stray
  By midnight, when tempestuous moons
Light them to many a shadowy prey,
  And earth beneath the thunder swoons.

— O who at any time hath seen
  Sight all so fearful and so fair,
Unstricken at his heart with keen
  Whole envy in that hour to share

Their unknown curse and all the strength
  Of the wild thirsts and lusts they know,
The sharp joys sating them at length,
  The new and greater lusts that grow?

But who of mortals shall rehearse
  How fair and dreadfully they stand,
Each marked with an eternal curse,
  Alien from every kin and land?

— Along the bright and blasted heights
  Loudly their cloven footsteps ring!
Full on their fronts the lightning smites,
  And falls like some dazed baffled thing.

Now through the mountain clouds they break,
  With many a crest high-antlered, reared
Athwart the storm: now they outshake
  Fierce locks or manes, glossy and weird,

That sweep with sharp perpetual sound
  The arid heights where the snows drift,
And drag the slain pines to the ground,
  And all into the whirlwind lift

The heavy sinking slopes of shade
  From hidden hills of monstrous girth,
Till new unearthly lights have flayed
  The draping darkness from the earth.

Henceforth what hiding-place shall hide
  All hallowed spirits that in form
Of mortal stand beneath the wide
  And wandering pale eye of the storm?

The beadsman in his lonely cell
  Hath cast one boding timorous look
Toward the heights; then loud and well,
  —Kneeling before the open book—

All night he prayeth in one breath,
  Nor spareth now his sins to own:
And through his prayer he shuddereth
  To hear how loud the forests groan.

For all abroad the lightnings reign,
  And rally, with their lurid spell,
The multitudinous campaign
  Of hosts not yet made fast in hell:

And us indeed no common arm,
  Nor magic of the dark may smite,
But, through all elements of harm,
  Across the strange fields of the night—

Enrolled with the whole giant host
  Of shadowy, cloud-outstripping things
Whose vengeful spells are uppermost,
  And convoyed by unmeasured wings,

We foil the thin dust of fatigue
  With bright-shod phantom feet that dare
All pathless places and the league
  Of the light shifting soils of air;

And loud, mid fearful echoings,
  Our throats, aroused with hell's own thirst,
Outbay the eternal trumpetings;
  The while, all impious and accurst,

BISCLAVARET

Revealed and perfected at length
  In whole and dire transfigurement,
With miracle of growing strength
  We win upon a keen warm scent.

Before us each cloud fastness breaks;
  And o'er slant inward wastes of light,
And past the moving mirage lakes,
  And on within the Lord's own sight —

We hunt the chosen of the Lord;
  And cease not, in wild course elate,
Until we see the flaming sword
  And Gabriel before His gate!

O many a fair and noble prey
  Falls bitterly beneath our chase;
And no man till the judgment day,
  Hath power to give these burial place;

But down in many a stricken home
  About the world, for these they mourn;
And seek them yet through Christendom
  In all the lands where they were born.

And oft, when hell's dread prevalence
  Is past, and once more to the earth
In chains of narrowed human sense
  We turn, — around our place of birth,

We hear the new and piercing wail;
  And, through the haunted day's long glare,
In fearful lassitudes turn pale
  With thought of all the curse we bear.

But, for long seasons of the moon,
  When the whole giant earth, stretched low,
Seems straightening in a silent swoon
  Beneath the close grip of the snow,

We well-nigh cheat the hideous spells
　　That force our souls resistless back,
With languorous torments worse than hell's
　　To the frail body's fleshly rack:

And with our brotherhood the storms,
　　Whose mighty revelry unchains
The avalanches, and deforms
　　The ancient mountains and the plains, —

We hold high orgies of the things,
　　Strange and accursèd of all flesh,
Whereto the quick sense ever brings
　　The sharp forbidden thrill afresh.

And far away, among our kin,
　　Already they account our place
With all the slain ones, and begin
　　The Masses for our soul's full grace.

Thought.

THERE is no place at all by night or day,
　　Where I — who am of that hard tyrant Thought
　　The slave — can find security in aught,
But He, almighty, reaching me, doth lay
His hand upon me there, so rough a way
　　Assaulting me, — however I am caught,
　　Walking or standing still — that for support
I sometimes lean on anything I may:
　　Then when he hath me, ease is none from him
Till he do out his strength with me; cold sweat
　　Comes o'er my body and on every limb;
　　My arm falls weak as from a fierce embrace;
And, ere he leaveth me, he will have set
　　A great eternal mark upon my face.

Palm Flowers.

IN a land of the sun's blessing,
　Where the passion-flower grows,
My heart keeps all worth possessing;
　And the way there no man knows.

—Unknown wonder of new beauty!
　There my Love lives all for me;
To love me is her whole duty,
　Just as I would have it be.

All the perfumes and perfections
　Of that clime have met with grace
In her body, and complexions
　Of its flowers are on her face.

All soft tints of flowers most vernal,
　Tints that make each other fade:
In her eyes they are eternal,
　Set in some mysterious shade.

Full of dreams are the abysses
　Of the night beneath her hair;
But an open dawn of kisses
　Is her mouth: O she is fair.

And she has so sweet a fashion
　With her languid loving eyes,
That she stirs my soul with passion,
　And renews my breath with sighs.

Now she twines her hair in tresses
　With some long red lustrous vine;
Now she weaves strange glossy dresses
　From the leafy fabrics fine:

23

And upon her neck there mingle
　Corals and quaint serpent charms,
And bright beaded sea-shells jingle,
　Set in circlets round her arms.

There—in solitudes sweet smelling,
　Where the mighty Banyan stands,
I and she have found a dwelling
　Shadowed by its giant hands:

All around our banyan bowers
　Shine the reddening palm-tree ranks
And the wild rare forest flowers
　Crowded on high purple banks.

Through the long enchanted weather
　—Ere the swollen fruits yet fall,
While red love-birds sit together
　In thick green, and voices call

From the hidden forest places,
　And are answered with strange shout
By the folk whose myriad faces
　All day long are peeping out

From shy loopholes all above us
　In the leafy hollows green,
—While all creatures seem to love us,
　And the lofty boughs are seen

Gilded and for ever haunted
　By the far ethereal smiles—
Through the long bright time enchanted,
　In those solitudes for miles,

I and She—at heart possessing
　Rhapsodies of tender thought—
Wander, till our thoughts too pressing
　Into new sweet words are wrought.

24

And at length, with full hearts sinking
  Back to silence and the maze
Of immeasurable thinking,
  In those inward forest ways,

We recline on mossy couches,
  Vanquished by mysterious calms,
All beneath the soothing touches
  Of the feather-leaved fan-palms.

Strangely, with a mighty hushing,
  Falls the sudden hour of noon;
When the flowers droop with blushing,
  And a deep miraculous swoon

Seems subduing the whole forest;
  Or some distant joyous rite
Draws away each bright-hued chorist:
  Then we yield with long delight

Each to each, our souls deep thirsting;
  And no sound at all is nigh,
Save from time to time the bursting
  Of some fire-fed fruit on high.

Then with sudden overshrouding
  Of impenetrable wings,
Comes the darkness and the crowding
  Mysteries of the unseen things.

O how happy are we lovers
  In weak wanderings hand in hand!—
Whom the immense palm forest covers
  In that strange enchanted land;

Whom its thousand sights stupendous
  Hold in breathless charmed suspense;
Whom its hidden sounds tremendous
  And its throbbing hues intense

And the mystery of each glaring
　Flower o'erwhelm with wonder dim;—
We, who see all things preparing
　Some Great Spirit's world for him!

Under pomps and splendid glamour
　Of the night skies limitless;
Through the weird and growing clamour
　Of the swaying wilderness;

Through each shock of sound that shivers
　The serene palms to their height,
By white rolling tongues of rivers
　Launched with foam athwart the night;

Lost and safe amid such wonders,
　We prolong our human bliss;
Drown the terrors of the thunders
　In the rapture of our kiss.

By some moon-haunted savanna,
　In thick scented mid-air bowers
Draped about with some liana,
　O what passionate nights are ours!

O'er our heads the squadron-dances
　Of the fire-fly wheel and poise;
And dim phantoms charm our trances,
　And link'd dreams prolong our joys—

Till around us creeps the early
　Sweet discordance of the dawn,
And the moonlight pales, and pearly
　Halos settle round the morn;

And from remnants of the hoary
　Mists, where now the sunshine glows,
Starts at length in crimson glory
　Some bright flock of flamingoes.

　　.　　.　　.　　.　　　.

O that land where the suns linger
  And the passion-flowers grow
Is the land for me the Singer:
  There I made me, years ago,

Many a golden habitation,
  Full of things most fair to see;
And the fond imagination
  Of my heart dwells there with me.

Now, farewell, all shameful sorrow!
  Farewell, troublous world of men!
I shall meet you on some morrow,
  But forget you quite till then.

John the Baptist.

(From "The Daughter of Herodias.")

I think he had not heard of the far towns;
Nor of the deeds of men, nor of kings' crowns;
  Before the thought of God took hold of him,
As he was sitting dreaming in the calm
  Of one first noon, upon the desert's rim,
Beneath the tall fair shadows of the palm,
All overcome with some strange inward balm.

He numbered not the changes of the year,
The days, the nights, and he forgot all fear
  Of death: each day he thought there should have been
A shining ladder set for him to climb
  Athwart some opening in the heavens, e'en
To God's eternity, and see, sublime —
His face whose shadow passing fills all time.

27

But he walked through the ancient wilderness.
O, there the prints of feet were numberless
    And holy all about him! And quite plain
He saw each spot an angel silvershod
    Had lit upon; where Jacob too had lain
The place seemed fresh, — and, bright and lately trod,
A long track showed where Enoch walked with God.

And often, while the sacred darkness trailed
Along the mountains smitten and unveiled
    By rending lightnings, — over all the noise
Of thunders and the earth that quaked and bowed
    From its foundations — he could hear the voice
Of great Elias prophesying loud
To Him whose face was covered by a cloud.

Salome.

(*From "The Daughter of Herodias."*)

HER long black hair danced round her like a snake
Allured to each charmed movement she did make;
    Her voice came strangely sweet;
She sang, "O, Herod, wilt thou look on me —
Have I no beauty thy heart cares to see?"
And what her voice did sing her dancing feet
    Seemed ever to repeat.

She sang, "O, Herod, wilt thou look on me?
What sweet I have, I have it all for thee;"
    And through the dance and song
She freed and floated on the air her arms
Above dim veils that hid her bosom's charms:
The passion of her singing was so strong
    It drew all hearts along.

28

SALOME

Her sweet arms were unfolded on the air,
They seemed like floating flowers the most fair—
    White lilies the most choice;
And in the gradual bending of her hand
There lurked a grace that no man could withstand;
Yea, none knew whether hands, or feet, or voice,
    Most made his heart rejoice.

The veils fell round her like thin coiling mists
Shot through by topaz suns, and amethysts,
    And rubies she had on;
And out of them her jewelled body came,
And seemed to all quite like a slender flame
That curled and glided, and that burnt and shone
    Most fair to look upon.

Then she began, on that well-polished floor,
Whose stones seemed taking radiance more and more
    From steps too bright to see,
A certain measure that was like some spell
Of winding magic, wherein heaven and hell
Were joined to lull men's souls eternally
    In some mid ecstasy:

For it was so inexplicably wrought
Of soft alternate motions, that she taught
    Each sweeping supple limb,
And in such intricate and wondrous ways
With bendings of her body, that the praise
Lost breath upon men's lips, and all grew dim
    Save her so bright and slim.

And through the swift mesh'd serpents of her hair
That lash'd and leapt on each place white and fair
    Of bosom or of arm,
And through the blazing of the numberless
And whirling jewelled fires of her dress,
Her perfect face no passion could disarm
    Of its reposeful charm.

Her head oft drooped as in some languid death
Beneath brim tastes of joy, and her rich breath
    Heaved faintly from her breast;
Her long eyes, opened fervently and wide,
Did seem with endless rapture to abide
In some fair trance through which the soul possest
    Love, ecstasy, and rest.

The Fountain of Tears.

I F you go over desert and mountain,
    Far into the country of sorrow,
    To-day and to-night and to-morrow,
And maybe for months and for years;
    You shall come, with a heart that is bursting
    For trouble and toiling and thirsting,
You shall certainly come to the fountain
At length, — to the Fountain of Tears.

Very peaceful the place is, and solely
    For piteous lamenting and sighing,
    And those who come living or dying
Alike from their hopes and their fears;
    Full of cypress-like shadows the place is,
    And statues that cover their faces:
But out of the gloom springs the holy
And beautiful Fountain of Tears.

And it flows and it flows with a motion
    So gentle and lovely and listless,
    And murmurs a tune so resistless
To him who hath suffered and hears —
    You shall surely — without a word spoken,
    Kneel down there and know your heart broken,
And yield to the long curb'd emotion
That day by the Fountain of Tears.

For it grows and it grows, as though leaping
  Up higher the more one is thinking;
  And ever its tunes go on sinking
More poignantly into the ears:
    Yea, so blessèd and good seems that fountain,
    Reached after dry desert and mountain,
You shall fall down at length in your weeping
And bathe your sad face in the tears.

Then, alas! while you lie there a season,
  And sob between living and dying,
  And give up the land you were trying
To find mid your hopes and your fears;
    — O the world shall come up and pass o'er you;
    Strong men shall not stay to care for you,
Nor wonder indeed for what reason
Your way should seem harder than theirs.

But perhaps, while you lie, never lifting
  Your cheek from the wet leaves it presses,
  Nor caring to raise your wet tresses
And look how the cold world appears, —
    O perhaps the mere silences round you —
    All things in that place grief hath found you,
Yea, e'en to the clouds o'er you drifting,
May soothe you somewhat through your tears.

You may feel, when a falling leaf brushes
  Your face, as though some one had kissed you;
  Or think at least some one who missed you
Hath sent you a thought, — if that cheers;
    Or a bird's little song, faint and broken,
    May pass for a tender word spoken:
— Enough, while around you there rushes
That life-drowning torrent of tears.

And the tears shall flow faster and faster,
  Brim over, and baffle resistance,
  And roll down bleared roads to each distance

Of past desolation and years;
  Till they cover the place of each sorrow,
  And leave you no past and no morrow:
For what man is able to master
And stem the great Fountain of Tears?

But the floods of the tears meet and gather;
  The sound of them all grows like thunder:
  —O into what bosom, I wonder,
Is poured the whole sorrow of years?
  For Eternity only seems keeping
  Account of the great human weeping:
May God then, the Maker and Father —
May He find a place for the tears!

The Spectre of the Past.

ON the great day of my life—
  On the memorable day —
Just as the long inward strife
  Of the echoes died away,
  Just as on my couch I lay
  Thinking thought away;
Came a Man into my room,
Bringing with him gloom.

Midnight stood upon the clock,
  And the street sound ceased to rise;
Suddenly, and with no knock,
  Came that Man before my eyes:
  Yet he seemed not anywise
  My heart to surprise,
And he sat down to abide
At my fireside.

But he stirred within my heart
  Memories of the ancient days;
And strange visions seemed to start
  Vividly before my gaze,
    Yea, from the most distant haze
    Of forgotten ways:
And he looked on me the while
With a most strange smile.

But my heart seemed well to know
  That his face the semblance had
Of my own face long ago
  Ere the years had made it sad,
    When my youthful looks were clad
    In a smile half glad;
To my heart he seemed in truth
All my vanished youth.

Then he named me by a name
  Long since unfamiliar grown,
But remembered for the same
  That my childhood's ears had known;
    And his voice was like my own
    In a sadder tone
Coming from the happy years
Choked, alas, with tears.

And, as though he nothing knew
  Of that day's fair triumphing,
Or the Present were not true,
  Or not worth remembering,
    All the Past he seemed to bring
    As a piteous thing
Back upon my heart again,
Yea, with a great pain:

33

"Do you still remember the winding street
    In the grey old village?" he seemed to say;
"And the long school days that the sun made sweet
    And the thought of the flowers from far away?
And the faces of friends whom you used to meet
    In that village day by day,
— Ay, the face of this one or of that?" he said,
And the names he named were names of the dead
    Who all in the churchyard lay.

"And do you remember the far green hills;
    Or the long straight path by the side of the stream;
Or the road that led to the farm and the mills,
    And the fields where you oft used to wander or dream
Or follow each change of your childish wills
    Like the dance of some gay sunbeam?" —
Then, alas, from right weeping I could not refrain,
For indeed all those things I remembered again, —
    As of yesterday they did seem.

And I thought of a day in a far lost Spring,
    When the sun with a kiss set the wild flowers free;
When my heart felt the kiss and the shadowy wing
    Of some beautiful spirit of things to be,
Who breathed in the song that the wild birds sing
    Some deep tender meaning for me, —
Who undid a strange spell in the world as it were,
Who set wide sweet whispers abroad in the air, —
    Made a presence I could not see.

"O for what have you wandered so far — so long?"
    Said the voice that was e'en as my voice of old:
"O for what have you done to the Past such wrong?
    Was there no fair dream on your own threshold?
In your childhood's home was there no fresh song?
    — Was your heart then all so cold?

Why, at length, are you weary and lone and sad,
But for casting away all the good that you had
  With the peace that was yours of old?

"Have you wholly forgotten the words you said,
  When you stood by a certain mound of earth,
When you vowed with your heart that that place you made
  The last burial-place for your love and your mirth,
For the pure past blisses you therein laid
  Were surely your whole life's worth?—
O, the angels who deck the lone graves with their tears
Have cared for this, morning and evening, for years,
  But of yours there has been long dearth:

"In the pure pale sheen of a hallowed night,
  When the graves are looking their holiest,
You may see it more glistering and more bright
  And holier-looking than all the rest;
You may see that the dews and the stars' strange light
  Are loving that grave the best;
But, perhaps, if you went in the clear noon-day,
After so many years you might scarce find the way
  Ere you tired indeed of the quest:

"For the path that leads to it is almost lost;
  And quite tall grass-flowers of sickly blue
Have grown up there and gathered for years, and tost
  Bitter germs all around them to grow up too;
For indeed all these years not a man has crost
  That pathway—not even You!"—
But alas! for these words to my heart he sent,
For I knew it was Marguérite's grave that he meant,
  And I felt that the words were true.

35

Love after Death.

THERE is an earthly glimmer in the Tomb:
  And, healed in their own tears and with long sleep,
  My eyes unclose and feel no need to weep;
But, in the corner of the narrow room,
Behold Love's spirit standeth, with the bloom
  That things made deathless by Death's self may keep.
  O what a change! for now his looks are deep,
And a long patient smile he can assume:
While Memory, in some soft low monotone,
  Is pouring like an oil into mine ear
  The tale of a most short and hollow bliss,
That I once throbbed indeed to call my own,
  Holding it hardly between joy and fear,—
  And how that broke, and how it came to this.

36

FROM
"MUSIC AND MOONLIGHT"

Ode.

WE are the music makers,
  And we are the dreamers of dreams,
Wandering by lone sea-breakers,
  And sitting by desolate streams;—
World-losers and world-forsakers,
  On whom the pale moon gleams;
Yet we are the movers and shakers
  Of the world for ever, it seems.

With wonderful deathless ditties
We build up the world's great cities,
  And out of a fabulous story
  We fashion an empire's glory:
One man with a dream, at pleasure,
  Shall go forth and conquer a crown;
And three with a new song's measure
  Can trample a kingdom down.

We, in the ages lying
  In the buried past of the earth,
Built Nineveh with our sighing,
  And Babel itself in our mirth;
And o'erthrew them with prophesying
  To the old of the new world's worth;
For each age is a dream that is dying,
  Or one that is coming to birth.

Song.

I made another garden, yea,
  For my new love;
I left the dead rose where it lay,
  And set the new above.

39

Why did the summer not begin?
  Why did my heart not haste?
My old love came and walked therein,
  And laid the garden waste.

She entered with her weary smile,
  Just as of old;
She looked around a little while,
  And shivered at the cold.
Her passing touch was death to all,
  Her passing look a blight:
She made the white rose-petals fall,
  And turned the red rose white.

Her pale robe, clinging to the grass,
  Seemed like a snake
That bit the grass and ground, alas!
  And a sad trail did make.
She went up slowly to the gate;
  And there, just as of yore,
She turned back at the last to wait,
  And say farewell once more.

Song.

HAS summer come without the rose,
  Or left the bird behind?
Is the blue changed above thee,
  O world! or am I blind?
Will you change every flower that grows,
  Or only change this spot,
Where she who said, I love thee,
  Now says, I love thee not?

The skies seemed true above thee,
  The rose true on the tree;
The bird seemed true the summer through,
  But all proved false to me.

40

World! is there one good thing in you,
  Life, love, or death — or what?
Since lips that sang, I love thee,
  Have said, I love thee not?

I think the sun's kiss will scarce fall
  Into one flower's gold cup;
I think the bird will miss me,
  And give the summer up.
O sweet place! desolate in tall
  Wild grass, have you forgot
How her lips loved to kiss me,
  Now that they kiss me not?

Be false or fair above me,
  Come back with any face,
Summer! — do I care what you do?
  You cannot change one place —
The grass, the leaves, the earth, the dew,
  The grave I make the spot —
Here, where she used to love me,
  Here, where she loves me not.

Song.

I went to her who loveth me no more,
  And prayed her bear with me, if so she might;
For I had found day after day too sore,
  And tears that would not cease night after night.
And so I prayed her, weeping, that she bore
To let me be with her a little; yea,
  To soothe myself a little with her sight,
Who loved me once, ah! many a night and day.

Then she who loveth me no more, maybe
  She pitied somewhat: and I took a chain
To bind myself to her, and her to me;
  Yea, so that I might call her mine again.

Lo! she forbade me not; but I and she
Fettered her fair limbs, and her neck more fair,
    Chained the fair wasted white of love's domain,
And put gold fetters on her golden hair.

Oh! the vain joy it is to see her lie
    Beside me once again; beyond release,
Her hair, her hand, her body, till she die,
    All mine, for me to do with as I please!
For, after all, I find no chain whereby
To chain her heart to love me as before,
    Nor fetter for her lips, to make them cease
From saying still she loveth me no more.

Song of Palms.

MIGHTY, luminous, and calm
Is the country of the palm,
    Crowned with sunset and sunrise,
    Under blue unbroken skies,
Waving from green zone to zone,
Over wonders of its own;
Trackless, untraversed, unknown,
    Changeless through the centuries.

Who can say what thing it bears?
    Blazing bird and blooming flower,
Dwelling there for years and years,
    Hold the enchanted secret theirs:
Life and death and dream have made
Mysteries in many a shade,
Hollow haunt and hidden bower
Closed alike to sun and shower.

Who is ruler of each race
Living in each boundless place,
    Growing, flowering, and flying,
    Glowing, revelling, and dying?

Wave-like, palm by palm is stirred,
And the bird sings to the bird,
And the day sings one rich word,
    And the great night comes replying.

Long red reaches of the cane,
Yellow winding water-lane,
    Verdant isle and amber river,
Lisp and murmur back again,
    And ripe under-worlds deliver
Rapturous souls of perfume, hurled
    Up to where green oceans quiver
In the wide leaves' restless world.

Many thousand years have been,
And the sun alone hath seen,
    Like a high and radiant ocean,
    All the fair palm world in motion;
But the crimson bird hath fed
With its mate of equal red,
    And the flower in soft explosion
With the flower hath been wed.

And its long luxuriant thought
Lofty palm to palm hath taught,
    While a single vast liana
All one brotherhood hath wrought,
    Crossing forest and savannah,
Binding fern and coco-tree,
    Fig-tree, buttress-tree, banana,
Dwarf cane and tall maríti.

Azure Islands.

SHIPMEN, sailing by night and day,
    High on the azure sea,
Do you not meet upon your way,
    Joyous and swift and free,

43

Sailing, sailing, ever sailing,
  Nigh to the western skylands,
My soul, a bark beyond your hailing,
  Bound for the azure islands?

When halcyon spells are on the wave,
  And in the enchanted sight
A path the dappling sunbeams pave
  Grows to intensest light;
And down in blue dominions, vainly
  Now the sea-sprite's wonder,
The sunken cities glitter plainly,
  And murmur in hushed thunder:

When every little billow breaks
  Into a liquid bloom,
And sings for one changed soul that wakes,
  Glad in so sweet a tomb;
And when in the rich horizon's dimness,
  Over the ocean revel,
Some blue land with a palm's crowned slimness
  Looms at the sea-waves' level:

I reach them as the wave wanes low,
  Leaving its stranded ores,
And evening-floods of amber glow
  And sleep around their shores;
Then, with a bird's will, a wind's power,
  My soul dwells there ecstatic,
Knowing each palm-tree and each flower,
  Gorgeous and enigmatic.

It plunges through some perfumed brake,
  Or depth of odorous shade,
That walls and roofs a dim hushed lake,
  Where endless dreams have stayed;

44

And there it takes the incarnation
　Of some amphibious blossom,
And lies in long-drawn contemplation,
　Buoyed on the water's bosom.

And mingling in the mysteries
　Of interchanging hues,　　·
And songs and sighs and silences,
　That in one magic fuse,
My soul my solitude enriches
　Through that profuse creation
With many a bird's impassioned speeches,
　Or a flower's emanation.

O gorgeous Erumango! isle
　Or blossom of the sea!
Often, some long enchanted while,
　Have I been part of thee;
Part of some saffron hue that lingers
　Above thy sapphire mountains;
One of thy spice-groves' full-voiced singers;
　One of thy murmuring fountains.

Zuleika.

ZULEIKA is fled away,
　Though your bolts and your bars were strong;
A minstrel came to the gate to-day
　And stole her away with a song.
His song was subtle and sweet,
It made her young heart beat,
　It gave a thrill to her faint heart's will,
And wings to her weary feet.

Zuleika was not for ye,
　Though your laws and your threats were hard;
The minstrel came from beyond the sea,
　And took her in spite of your guard:

His ladder of song was slight,
But it reached to her window height;
  Each verse so frail was the silken rail
From which her soul took flight.

The minstrel was fair and young;
  His heart was of love and fire;
His song was such as you ne'er have sung,
  And only love could inspire:
He sang of the singing trees,
And the passionate sighing seas,
  And the lovely land of his minstrel band;
And with many a song like these

He drew her forth to the distant wood,
  Where bird and flower were gay,
And in silent joy each green tree stood;
  And with singing along the way
He drew her to where each bird
Repeated his magic word,
  And there seemed a spell she could not tell
In every sound she heard.

And singing and singing still,
  He lured her away so far,
Past so many a wood and valley and hill,
  That now, would you know where they are?
In a bark on a silver stream,
As fair as you see in a dream;
  Lo! the bark glides along to the minstrel's song,
While the smooth waves ripple and gleam.

And soon they will reach the shore
  Of that land whereof he sings,
And love and song will be evermore
  The precious, the only things;

They will live and have long delight,
They two in each other's sight,
 In the violet vale of the nightingale,
And the flower that blooms by night.

Song.

NOW I am on the earth,
 What sweet things love me?
Summer, that gave me birth,
 And glows on still above me;
The bird I loved a little while;
 The rose I planted;
The woman in whose golden smile
 Life seems enchanted.

Now I am in the grave,
 What sweet things mourn me?
Summer, that all joys gave,
 Whence death, alas! hath torn me;
One bird that sang to me; one rose
 Whose beauty moved me;
One changeless woman; yea, all those
 That living loved me.

In Love's Eternity.

MY body was part of the sun and the dew,
 Not a trace of my death to me clave,
There was scarce a man left on the earth whom I knew,
 And another was laid in my grave.
I was changed and in heaven, the great sea of blue
 Had long washed my soul pure in its wave.

My sorrow was turned to a beautiful dress,
  Very fair for my weeping was I;
And my heart was renewed, but it bore none the less
  The great wound that had brought me to die,
The deep wound that She gave who wrought all my distress;
  Ah, my heart loved her still in the sky!

I wandered alone where the stars' tracks were bright;
  I was beauteous and holy and sad;
I was thinking of her who of old had the might
  To have blest me, and made my death glad;
I remembered how faithless she was, and how light,
  Yea, and how little pity she had.

My soul had forgiven each separate tear,
  She had bitterly wrung from my eyes;
But I thought of her lightness,—ah! sore was my fear
  She would fall somewhere never to rise,
And that no one would love her, to bring her soul near
  To the heavens, where love never dies.

She had drawn me with feigning, and held me a day;
  She had taken the passionate price
That my heart gave for love, with no doubt or delay,
  For I thought that her smile would suffice;
She had played with and wasted and then cast away
  The true heart that could never love twice.

And false must she be; she had followed the cheat
  That ends loveless and hopeless below:
I remembered her words' cruel worldly deceit
  When she bade me forget her and go.
She could ne'er have believed after death we might meet,
  Or she would not have let me die so.

I thought, and was sad: the blue fathomless seas
  Bore the white clouds in luminous throng;
And the souls that had loved were in each one of these;

They passed by with a great upward song:
They were going to wander beneath the fair trees,
In high Eden — their joy would be long.

How sweet to look back to that desolate space
   When the heaven scarce my heaven seemed!
She came suddenly, swiftly, — a great healing grace
   Filled her features, and forth from her streamed.
With a cry our lips met, and a long close embrace
   Made the past like a thing I had dreamed.

"Ah, Love!" she began, "when I found you were dead,
   I was changed, and the world was changed too;
On a sudden I felt that the sunshine had fled,
   And the flowers and summer gone too;
Life but mocked me; I found there was nothing instead
   But to turn back and weep all in you.

"When you were not there to fall down at my feet,
   And pour out the whole passionate store
Of the heart that was made to make my heart complete,
   In true words that my memory bore, —
Then I found that those words were the only words sweet,
   And I knew I should hear them no more.

"Ah, yes! but your love was a fair magic toy,
   That you gave to a child, who scarce deigned
To glance at it — forsook it for some passing joy,
   Never guessing the charm it contained;
But you gave it and left it, and none could destroy
   The fair talisman where it remained.

"And, surely, no child, but a woman at last
   Found your gift where the child let it lie,
Understood the whole secret it held, sweet and vast,
   The fair treasure a world could not buy;
And believed not the meaning could ever have past,
   Any more than the giver could die."

49

She ceased. To my soul's deepest sources the sense
   Of her words with a full healing crept,
And my heart was delivered with rapture intense
   From the wound and the void it had kept;
Then I saw that her heart was a heaven immense
   As my love; and together we wept.

To a Young Murderess.

FAIR yellow murderess, whose gilded head
   Gleaming with deaths; whose deadly body white,
Writ o'er with secret records of the dead;
   Whose tranquil eyes, that hide the dead from sight
Down in their tenderest depth and bluest bloom;
   Whose strange unnatural grace, whose prolonged youth,
Are for my death now and the shameful doom
   Of all the man I might have been in truth,

Your fell smile, sweetened still, lest I might shun
   Its lingering murder, with a kiss for lure,
Is like the fascinating steel that one
   Most vengeful in his last revenge, and sure
The victim lies beneath him, passes slow,
   Again and oft again before his eyes,
And over all his frame, that he may know
   And suffer the whole death before he dies.

Will you not slay me? Stab me; yea, somehow,
   Deep in the heart: say some foul word to last,
And let me hate you as I love you now.
   Oh, would I might but see you turn and cast
That false fair beauty that you e'en shall lose,
   And fall down there and writhe about my feet,
The crooked loathly viper I shall bruise
   Through all eternity: —
              Nay, kiss me, Sweet!

Greater Memory.

IN the heart there lay buried for years
Love's story of passion and tears;
Of the heaven that two had begun,
 And the horror that tore them apart,
When one was love's slayer, but one
 Made a grave for the love in his heart.

The long years passed weary and lone,
And it lay there and changed there unknown;
Then one day from its innermost place,
 In the shamed and the ruined love's stead,
Love arose with a glorified face,
 Like an angel that comes from the dead.

It uplifted the stone that was set
On that tomb which the heart held yet;
But the sorrow had mouldered within,
 And there came from the long closed door
A clear image, that was not the sin
 Or the grief that lay buried before.

The grief it was long washed away
In the weeping of many a day;
And the terrible past lay afar,
 Like a dream left behind in the night;
And the memory that woke was a star
 Shining pure in the soul's pure light.

There was never the stain of a tear
On the face that was ever so dear;
'Twas the same in each lovelier way;
 'Twas the old love's holier part,
And the dream of the earliest day
 Brought back to the desolate heart.

It was knowledge of all that had been
In the thought, in the soul unseen;
'Twas the word which the lips could not say
   To redeem and recover the past;
It was more than was taken away
   Which the heart got back at the last.

The passion that lost its spell,
The rose that died where it fell,
The look that was looked in vain,
   The prayer that seemed lost evermore,
They were found in the heart again,
   With all that the heart would restore.

And thenceforward the heart was a shrine
For that memory to dwell in divine,
Till from life, as from love, the dull leaven
   Of grief-stained earthliness fell;
And thenceforth in the infinite heaven
   That heart and that memory dwell.

FROM
"SONGS OF A WORKER"

Silences.

To ————————.

'TIS a world of silences. I gave a cry
  In the first sorrow my heart could not withstand;
I saw men pause, and listen, and look sad,
As though an answer in their hearts they had;
  Some turned away, some came and took my hand,
For all reply.

I stood beside a grave. Years had passed by;
  Sick with unanswered life I turned to death,
And whispered all my question to the grave,
And watched the flowers desolately wave,
  And grass stir on it with a fitful breath,
For all reply.

I raised my eyes to heaven; my prayer went high
  Into the luminous mystery of the blue;
My thought of God was purer than a flame
And God it seemed a little nearer came,
  Then passed; and greater still the silence grew,
For all reply.

But you! If I can speak before I die,
  I spoke to you with all my soul, and when
I look at you 'tis still my soul you see.
Oh, in your heart was there no word for me?
  All would have answered had you answered then
With even a sigh.

Lynmouth.

I have brought her I love to this sweet place,
　　Far away from the world of men and strife
That I may talk to her a charmèd space,
　　And make a long rich memory in my life.

Around my love and me the brooding hills,
　　Full of delicious murmurs, rise on high,
Closing upon this spot the summer fills,
　　And over which there rules the summer sky.

Behind us on the shore down there the sea
　　Roars roughly, like a fierce pursuing hound;
But all this hour is calm for her and me;
　　And now another hill shuts out the sound.

And now we breathe the odours of the glen,
　　And round about us are enchanted things;
The bird that hath blithe speech unknown to men,
　　The river keen, that hath a voice and sings.

The tree that dwells with one ecstatic thought,
　　Wider and fairer growing year by year,
The flower that flowereth and knoweth nought,
　　The bee that scents the flower and draweth near.

Our path is here; the rocky winding ledge
　　That sheer o'erhangs the rapid shouting stream
Now dips down smoothly to the quiet edge,
　　Where restful waters lie as in a dream.

The green exuberant branches overhead
　　Sport with the golden magic of the sun,
Here quite shut out, here like rare jewels shed
　　To fright the glittering lizards as they run.

And wonderful are all those mossy floors
   Spread out beneath us in some pathless place,
Where the sun only reaches and outpours
   His smile, where never a foot hath left a trace.

And there are perfect nooks that have been made
   By the long-growing tree, through some chance turn
Its trunk took; since transformed with scent and shade,
   And filled with all the glory of the fern.

And tender-tinted wood flowers are seen,
   Clear starry blooms and bells of pensive blue,
That lead their delicate lives there in the green—
   What were the world if it should lose their hue?

Even o'er the rough out-jutting stone that blocks
   The narrow way, some cunning hand hath strewn
The moss in rich adornment, and the rocks
   Down there seem written thick with many a rune.

And here, upon that stone, we rest awhile,
   For we can see the lovely river's fall,
And wild and sweet the place is to beguile
   My love, and keep her till I tell her all.

Song.

WHEN the Rose came I loved the Rose,
   And thought of none beside,
Forgetting all the other flowers,
   And all the others died;
And morn and noon, and sun and showers,
And all things loved the Rose,
   Who only half returned my love,
Blooming alike for those.

57

I was the rival of a score
　Of loves on gaudy wing,
The nightingale I would implore
　For pity not to sing;
Each called her his; still I was glad
　To wait or take my part;
I loved the Rose — who might have had
　The fairest lily's heart.

Eden.

WEARY and wandering, hand in hand,
　Through ways and cities rough,
And with a law in every land
　Written against our love,
We set our hearts to seek and find,
Forgotten now and out of mind,
　Lost Eden garden desolate,
Hoping the angel would be kind,
　And let us pass the gate.

We turned into the lawless waste
　Wild outer gardens of the world —
We heard awhile our footsteps chased,
　Men's curses at us hurled;
But safe at length, we came and found,
Open with ruined wall all round,
　Lost Eden garden desolate;
No angel stood to guard the ground
　At Eden garden gate.

We crossed the flower-encumbered floor,
　And wandered up and down the place,
And marvelled at the open door
　And all the desolate grace
And beast and bird with joy and song

58

That broke man's laws the whole day long;
  For all was free in Eden waste:
There seemed no rule of right and wrong,
  No fruit we might not taste.

Our hearts, o'erwhelmed with many a word
  Of bitter scathing, human blame,
Trembled with what they late had heard,
  And fear upon us came,
Till, finding the forbidden tree,
We ate the fruit, and stayed to see
  If God would chide our wickedness;
No God forbade my love and me
  In Eden wilderness.

The rose has overgrown the bower
  In lawless Eden garden waste,
The eastern flower and western flower
  Have met and interlaced;
The trees have joined above and twined
And shut out every cruel wind
  That from the world was blown:
Ah, what a place for love to find
  Is Eden garden grown!

The fair things exiled from the earth
  Have found the way there in a dream;
The phoenix has its fiery birth
  And nests there in the gleam;
Love's self, with draggled rainbow wings,
At rest now from his wanderings,
  In Eden beds and bowers hath lain
So long, no wealth of worldly kings
  Will win him back again.

And now we need not fear to kiss;
  The serpent is our playfellow,
And tempts us on from bliss to bliss,
  No man can see or know.

Love was turned out of Eden first
By God, and then of man accurst;
   And fleeing long from human hate,
And counting man's hard laws the worst,
    Returned to Eden gate.

Now every creature there obeys
   Exuberantly his lawless power;
The wall is overthrown, the ways
   Ruined by bird and flower;
The nuptial riot of the rose
Runs on for centuries and grows;
   The great heart of the place is strong—
It swells in overmastering throes
   Of passionate sigh and song.

And while we joy in Eden's state,
   Outside men serve a loveless lord;
They think the angel guards the gate
   With burning fiery sword!
Ah, fools! he fled an age ago,
The roses pressed upon him so,
   And all the perfume from within,
And he forgot or did not know;
   Eden must surely win.

Keeping a Heart.

To M——— D———.

IF one should give me a heart to keep,
   With love for the golden key,
The giver might live at ease or sleep;
It should ne'er know pain, be weary, or weep,
   The heart watched over by me.

I would keep that heart as a temple fair,
  No heathen should look therein;
Its chaste marmoreal beauty rare
I only should know, and to enter there
  I must hold myself from sin.

I would keep that heart as a casket hid
  Where precious jewels are ranged,
A memory each; as you raise the lid,
You think you love again as you did
  Of old, and nothing seems changed.

How I should tremble day after day,
  As I touched with the golden key,
Lest aught in the heart were changed, or say
That another had stolen one thought away
  And it did not open to me.

But ah, I should know that heart so well,
  As a heart so loving and true,
As a heart that I held with a golden spell,
That so long as I changed not I could foretell
  That heart would be changeless too.

I would keep that heart as the thought of heaven,
  To dwell in a life apart,
My good should be done, my gift be given,
In hope of the recompense there; yea, even
  My life should be led in that heart.

And so on the eve of some blissful day,
  From within we should close the door
On glimmering splendours of love, and stay
In that heart shut up from the world away,
  Never to open it more.

Prophetic Spring.

TO-DAY 'tis Spring; the hawthorn-tree
Is green with buds; to-day maybe
She whom I think of thinks of me,
    And finds the thought enough;
And when those buds are grown to leaves,
That thought wherein she scarce believes
    Will grow perhaps to love.

Soon as the flowers of May appear,
For love of me she will draw near,
And hoping, dreading, I shall hear
    Perhaps, and own my bliss.
Awhile beneath the hawthorn sweet
Our o'erstrained quickening hearts will beat,
Our purple thirsting mouths will meet
    And revel in their kiss.

But when pink May becomes red June,
And summer sounds a glorious tune,
Under some lordlier tree aswoon
    Together we shall lie.
And then to-day's half-timid thought,
May's thrill and kiss will seem as nought
To the full joy we shall have taught
    Each other, she and I.

If She But Knew.

IF she but knew that I am weeping
        Still for her sake,
That love and sorrow grow with keeping
        Till they must break

62

My heart that breaking will adore her,
    Be hers and die;
If she might hear me once implore her,
    Would she not sigh?

If she but knew that it would save me
    Her voice to hear,
Saying she pitied me, forgave me,
    Must she forbear?
If she were told that I was dying,
    Would she be dumb?
Could she content herself with sighing?
    Would she not come?

A Love Symphony.

ALONG the garden ways just now
    I heard the flowers speak;
The white rose told me of your brow,
    The red rose of your cheek;
The lily of your bended head,
    The bindweed of your hair:
Each looked its loveliest and said
    You were more fair.

I went into the wood anon,
    And heard the wild birds sing
How sweet you were; they warbled on,
    Piped, trilled the self-same thing.
Thrush, blackbird, linnet, without pause,
    The burden did repeat,
And still began again because
    You were more sweet.

And then I went down to the sea,
    And heard it murmuring too,
Part of an ancient mystery,
    All made of me and you.

How many a thousand years ago
    I loved, and you were sweet —
Longer I could not stay, and so
    I fled back to your feet.

Fetters.

(After Sully Prudhomme.)

IN too much seeking love I found but grief;
    I have but multiplied the means of pain;
A thousand ties too poignant or too brief
    Bind me to things that love not back again.

All things with equal power my heart have won —
    Truth by its light, the Unknown by its veil —
A tenuous gold thread binds me to the sun,
    And to each star a silken thread more frail.

The cadence chains me to the melody,
    Its velvet softness to the rose I touch;
One smile soon robbed my eye of liberty,
    And for my mouth the first kiss did as much.

My life now hangs upon these fragile threads,
    Captive of all fair things I feel or see;
Each breath that change or trouble o'er them sheds
    Rends from my heart itself a part of me.

The Appointment.

(After Sully Prudhomme.)

'TIS late; the astronomer in his lonely height,
    Exploring all the dark, descries afar
    Orbs that like distant isles of splendour are,
And mornings whitening in the infinite.

64

Like winnowed grain the worlds go by in flight,
  Or swarm in glistening spaces nebular;
  He summons one dishevelled wandering star;
"Return ten centuries hence on such a night."
The star will come. It dare not by one hour
  Cheat Science or falsify her calculation;
Men will have passed, but watchful in the tower
  Man shall remain in sleepless contemplation.
And should all men have perished there in turn,
Truth in their place would watch that star's return.

FROM

"LAYS OF FRANCE"

(*Founded on the Lays of Marie.*)

Two Songs.

1.

O Love, where is the bed we made
  In scented wood-ways for sweet sin?
The sun was with us and the shade;
  The warm blue covered us in:

All men their curse on us had laid—
  Finding had slain us both therein;
But, summer with us, not afraid
  Were we to love and sin.

O Love, the crushed place is quite fair;
Leaves have sprung back and flowers grown there;
  The blithe trees no long record bore;
  The flown bird knoweth no more;

The hard one never found our lair;—
We are not slain, Love,—we are fair,
  And love, ay, as we loved before:
  —Let us go back once more!

2.

WOULD I might go far over sea,
  My Love, or high above the air,
And come to land or heaven with thee,
Where no law is and none shall be
  Against beholding the most rare
Strange beauty that thou hast for me.

Alas, for, in this bitter land,
Full many a written curse doth stand
  Against the kiss thy lips should bear;
Against the sweet gift of thy hand;
  Against the knowing that thou art fair,
  And too fond loving of thy hair!

69

Chaitivel;

or, the

Lay of Love's Unfortunate.

LADIES and lovers, may ye dwell
   In joy; yea, now and after me;
And, for all I shall sing or tell,
Hold me but one who loveth well,
   And singeth of mere joy to see
His lady's golden loveliness, —
Yea, joyeth, and may scarce repress
The song he hath for every tress
   Her hand hath braided or set free —
The rush of rapturous words that break
Frail wings against his lips and take
   A songless death, for mere delight
   In that fresh miracle of white
And perfect red and perfect gold
Each new day brings him to behold
   Renewed and yet unchanged in her.
   Whence are the rosy seas that stir
With richly glowing wave of thin
Ethereal fire, alway within,
   Alway about her heart — all day
Flooding the extreme flower of lip
And finger-tip and bosom-tip, —
   As summer, flooding in such way
   Earth, air and heaven, will seem to stay
Gathered up richly in the last
   And least of the last rose? — O whence
Is all her wonder, never past,
Nor ever dwelt with and possest
   Quite through, bewildering the sense
   With loving, looking and suspense

Of loving;—shapeless shades and swift
Transfiguration of heavens that drift
 Ever with glory giving place
 To glory on her form and face?—
Yea, infinite of change and light
And wide uncomprehended sight
 Seems every way his lady's grace,—
As seemeth to the day and night
 Some infinite world of flowers, transformed
By unseen wands of wind. And he,
Beholding, loves; but may not see
Or know whence aught of her may be:
 Only, beholding, he hath formed,
Ah, many a song for very love
Of her and wonder. But, above,
 —Yea, quite beyond the rapturous days
He leads with her, he thinketh well
 Some heaven with fair untrodden ways
Shall ever be for him to dwell
 Rejoicing in her, learning praise
More passionate of her, winning whole
Immortal knowledge of her soul.

Ladies and lovers, will ye see
How gold hair hath its perjury?
 And how the lip may twice or thrice
Undo the soul; and how the heart
 May quite annul the heart's own price
Given for many a goodly part
 Of heaven? How one love shall be fair,
 And whole and perfect in the rare
Great likeness of an angel,—yea,
 And how another, golden-miened,
With lovely seeming and sweet way,
 Shall come and be but as a fiend
To tempt and drag the soul away—

71

And all for ever? Listen well:
This is a lay of heaven and hell:
Listen, and think how it shall be
With you in love's eternity.

Some age ago, love's splendid lures
   Through the enchanted world made fair
   Each woman's soft enamouring snare;
And the contagion that endures
   Among men's hearts spread everywhere
Love's ailing that love only cures;
And, far as the unblemished fire
   Flooded down joyous from the sun
Caused rapturous living and desire
   Unearthly in the earth, not one
   Of fair mankind was free to shun
The sudden endless fate of flame
   Caught in the hazard of a look
Crossing a kindled look. The same
   Frail human life it was that shook
With the immortal burning soul
   Of love traversing it, consumed
With bearing inwardly the whole
Of some celestial joy, or sole
   — In fair midst of the world that bloomed
Or withered — through the long sharp throe
Of some inexplicable woe
   Reaching out to a shoreless sea
Of sadness after death. The earth
   Was beautiful with flower and tree,
And full of the delicious mirth
   And low soft endless jubilee
   Of bird and nameless creature free
To feel the sun; and, where the grave
   Saddened and broke the last year's green,
There most was this year's summer brave
   With glorious flower and fresh with keen

New scent. And men and women, thrilled
  With their own passionate thoughts unseen,
Went fair about the fair world, filled
  With wondrous joy or misery
Killing them at the heart; beheld
  The sun, and looked upon the sky,
  And saw the flowers, and felt go by
The summer; and were not changed, but held
  Their secret of eternity
Within them. And the earth was glad,
Whether the heart was blithe or sad.

But Sarrazine, of whom I sing,
Had shut her soul up from each thing
  That once with all her soul she knew
  Sweet in the earth, bright in the blue;
And, joyless, in the midst between
Fair blue of heaven and green earth's green,
Lived now this lovely Sarrazine
  With passionate thinking and unknown
  Most secret flowering of her lone
And infinite beauty. All amazed
She was, and fearfully she gazed
  Into each dismal future year,
  The while it ceased not that a tear,
Born of her thought right wearily,
  Found its way backward to the drear
Dead ashes of some memory
  In a sweet fatal reckless past
  Love had made recklessly and cast
Against her soul.
                She did not die,
But dreamed and lived, and bade the grey
Of grieving, more and more each day,
Gather around and steal away
  Her hidden fairness, that was bloom
  More white and wondrous in that tomb

Where the sun touched it not, and sight
Should never worship, and delight
Flower not of it day or night.

The slow cloud found it sweet to rest
 Over each shadow-haunted tower
Of her lone castle, and to remain
Low brooding over that domain
Of deep autumnal wood and plain
And mirroring lake that she possest;
 The sun and summer owned no flower
Down in the deep and wayward ways
 Ruined and lost about her bower,
Whose desolation was the nest
Of a strange plaintive bird with crest
Of tarnished fiery feathers. Haze
 Of changeless morn and noon was blue
 Above the still blue of the lake,
Where, year by year, some long dream grew
More and more wonderful, and threw
 A stranger spell over wild brake
And dripping mile of sallow sedge —
 Where the dark bittern and the crake
 Answered with lone unearthly cry,
Or spectral, on the oozy edge,
 Some tall grey egret with wide eye
Stood slumbering. Not a troubled thought
 Of toiling in the world, or deeds
Of living men, was ever brought
To break such magic as dreams wrought
 In that dim region; but the reeds,
And redolent snakelike flowers, and weeds
Trailed in the wave, and songless bird,
 With many a shadow thinly seen
And many a strange unseen thing heard
 To wander up and down between

74

The desolate sedges with drear sound —
All were become unearthly, bound
  In the enchanting solitude
  Of some vast supernatural mood
Of sadness. All had learned the heart
  Of Sarrazine; and every sore
Bewailing thought of hers was part
Of burdens that the silent things
  Of wave and fen and feather bore,
On languid leaves and drooping wings,
  In the blue stillness more and more
The haunt of cloud and dream.

And for his sake — who quite possest,
  In short blind life upon the earth,
The whole irrevocable gift
  Of her sweet body's passionate worth —
Whose soul was ever strong and swift
To seek her shaken soul and wrest
  Some irremediable word
Out of its troubled speech to drift
  Onward eternal and be heard
Among the destinies, — for him,
  She now had given up to grief,
To let grief ruin it and dim
  And waste it as worms do a leaf,
  The rich continual flowering
Of each white unregarded limb,
  Yea, and the whole of that rich thing,
Her woman's loveliness, that love
  Would perfect secretly and bring
To many a marble grace above
His wont. O how grief slew each day
  With deadliest remembering
  Of some first day the cruel past
Held golden with joy torn away
  For ever! Snake-like, how he cast

His sickly and bewildering coil
About her life, holding his prey,
Her heart, with fierce fang of regret,
    And making poisoned thought to spoil
Her desolate fairness with lone fret!

Now she would weary out the days,
    Joylessly looking on the white
Slim wonder that she was, whose praise
    Henceforth must be omitted quite
Out of men's praising mouths; whose sight
Should ne'er strike sudden with amaze
    One other heart fain to have crost
That solitude, where she must be
    Evermore as a flower lost
Or nameless unto men. To see
    The wild white lilies, passionless
And lonely, wasted in the rank
Green shadowy shallows of the bank,
    Was to see many a loveliness —
No more rejected and left out,
    As a thing none cared to possess
Of love and time — than, past all doubt,
    Her joyless form and face were now
Till death. Was the world whole without
    One need of her, one thought of how
Love prospered making her — one look
    At the short perfect miracle
His passionate hands wrought when they took
The rare sweet elements, the fine
    And delicate fires, and wove the spell
Of her rich being? Did days yet shine,
    And men love boundlessly and well
    In the fair world, beyond that cell
Of grey thoughts shutting out the sun
Her life seemed brought to? yea, since none

Set living heart upon her more,
And all she was and all she bore,
Of rare and wonderful lay known
To the worms only left alone
    With faded secrets in the core
Of dead men's hearts?

                        Time was so bare,
    — Her heart at solitary feast
Of sorrow sitting unreleast
For ever, wasting slow the hair
    Of gold, the plenteous form of white
    Unconquerable flower, through night
And day, that emptied year and year
Of sullied summers, drawing near
    To death scarce more a winter; — yea,

And one last chosen tomb seemed, day
And night, so little comforted
With summer given or true tear shed —
There might have been — her heart now said
    Sometimes all softly — even for him,
That earlier lover, lightly slain
    Without the touch of her for dim
Delicious dreaming after vain,
    Void life, the guiltless recompense
Of more love than he sought to save
    His soul; yea, though he had gone hence,
Telling the worms they should but have
    Hair's gold that once had been his bed,
    And dust that love for once had wed
To his glad dust, when death made her
Some next year's spoil! O who would stir
    In sleep down there, and think he missed
    Aught of the faultless mouth that kissed
His life all through? For, verily,
    — He who had all — was not his day,
    E'en to death softened endlessly

With love, filled to the full and more
  With sweet of hers? And, where he lay,
Was not the grave o'erbrimmed with store
Of perfect memories and rich ore
  Of a life rich in love? And, now,
  It seemed all bitter to avow
That one most gracious should have gone
Uncheered to death, who had lived on
  Right rapturously, if once his brow
Had felt her lips; if once his hand
  Had revelled on her, and his heart
  Filled itself with one lovely part
Of loveliness, the rotting sand
  Of time alone should use with kiss
  Joyless for ever. Would not this—
To weigh the lost wealth of her hair
  Once in his hand, as one might poise
Some weight of gold—have seemed right fair
  To him, amid the few sad joys
He thought it well to die for? Yea,
And now the whole sweet, that he lay
  Evermore thirsting for, was there
  At waste for ever, out of care
Of any; and no man came back
  To call it his.

           And, since to her
No man returned; since no more lack
  Of her gave any strength to stir
The very grave-stone and come back;
And he whose soul's least word of love
Seemed a love-fetter strong enough
  To bind eternity to whole
  Eternity,—since now his soul
Having content of her, or quite
  Forgetting, left her, as a thing
  Not owned, and never jealous sting

78

Caused him to care now, day or night,
What chance might happen to the white
  Unblemished beauty or the heart
  His empire:—ah, as houseless wraiths
And unhoused creeping beasts would glide
Back to a house the day he died
  Who cast them forth,—so, from each part
  Of her annulled past, full of faiths
Abjured and fruitless loves and loss,
  There came back to her heart the host
  Of memories comfortless; the ghost
Of every lover now might cross
  Its threshold when he would, to scare
  And grieve her with his tears, or bare
The great wound in his heart, or make
Long threat of unknown things for sake
  Of some forgotten heedless word.

  It seemed now as a sad thing heard
But yesterday, how, bearing still
Fair vow of hers, wherefrom the will
  Of other love had wrenched her, yea,
Relying ever on each fair
  Uncancelled word, and, night and day,
Bound, with her gift of golden hair,
  To hold hers only heart and hand,
  For ever,—one in Paynim land
Died loving her. The intense flower
  Of waving strange-leaved trees that sang
  His dirge with voices wild and soft,
Wafted her perfume that had power
  To shake her heart; warm air, that rang
  With ends of unknown singing, oft
Broke in upon her, as though space
  Of cold climes and cold seas between
  Were dwindling, and she should have seen
That fair unconsecrated place,

79

Golden in sunlight, green in shade
Of many a palm and mighty blade
Of monstrous herb.
                              Yea, these were three
Whose lives and deaths were hers; and she
    Had only given good to one;
And all were with her now, to share
And haunt her thoughts quite to the bare
    Lone end of living. There was none
Among sweet women whose ripe heart,
Full of the perfect precious part
    Of many a love, was a deep tomb
    Where fair dead lay in goodly gloom
More royally than these, whose fate
    Was filled and ended in her, lay
In her proud heart, disconsolate
    And lonely, turning from the day
    Into its own rich grieving grey.

But in the separate place that death
    Had found for him, to rest from life,
    To dream upon it, or to wait,
Each of her lovers held the breath
    Of his strong dauntless spirit rife
    With memories; or content with late
Fair kisses on his mouth; or sure
Of heaven because of some sweet lure
    Of looks or pledge or perfect vow
She made him, — doubting her not his
For ever in fair destinies.

    He who ne'er felt upon his brow
The perfect blessing of her kiss,
    Stayed his long thirst with thinking how
Some early and far-reaching smile,
That looked on many a distant mile
    Of golden promise, seemed to bind
    His love to follow her and find

Dim outskirts of her life to cling
  With solace in; and, where the chill
And changeless dark spread covering
  His patient soul, he thought it still
  Her shadow on him; and a thrill   .
That was not joyless turned the sting
Of death.
        And he who, in the fair
Rich Paynim place, with the ripe glare
  Of foreign summers gilding palm
  And poisonous fruit about him, calm
And mighty, rusted in red steel—
Not merely barren did he feel
  Death's prison and the silent gloom
  Around him; but, within, the tomb
Was opulent with a glimmering gold;
  For the slim tress that once was hid
Upon his heart, was grown to fold
On fold that many times had rolled
  About him; and he lay amid
The splendours of it, and thought well
That he should have her soul for hell
  Or heaven.
           But he who had all sweet
Latest and longest of her,—day
And night and many a year he lay,
  Enthralled, past knowing cold or heat
  Or hearing thunder or the feet
Of armies, in a long deep dream
  Of her sweet body, full of joy
And magical amaze and gleam
Of endless excellence; there nought
  Might reach his spirit or destroy
Its passionate raptures of long thought,
—Save only if, beneath God's sky,
  One other creature should draw nigh
To touching her whom his soul bought.

Tranquil, and holding it enow
  Each of them had his hope or bliss
  Or memory of her; and with this
He lay alone there,—as I trow,
Thinking that she was only his.

—O men and women, Love is king
Upon the earth; summer and spring
  Will serve him in the year to come
With all new rapture, when the blast
Of many a long-drawn autumn day,
  Made golden with fair thought and dumb
Remembering of the perfect past,
Shall have swept utterly away
  The dry dead leaves of summer and spring
  That spent themselves with worshipping
His latest godhead perfectly:
His realms are all the lands that lie
Beneath yon distant unknown sky—
  Where only freed souls go unseen
  To different dooms: his are the green
Of grass, the blue of seas, the red
  Of passionate roses,—each frail life
  Of rose and bird and slight thing rife
With sunlight is but sweetly led
  By him to its sweet life and death.
  But, more than all, while ye have breath
And rosy relic of the rose
  Born with you—men and women, lo,
  Your rich eternal hearts that grow
Like widening flowers that cannot close
  Their leaves—are Love's, to turn and use,
  And work upon as he may choose.

Do ye not feel how love pursues
  Your full hearts ever with his new
Inconstant summer—to convert
  And steal them from the thing they knew

Their own, — to cause them to desert
　　Their piteous memories and the few
Fond faiths of perfect years? Alas,
He careth not how he may hurt
　　The dead, or trouble them that wait
In heaven, so he may bring to pass
　　Ever some new thing passionate
And sweet upon the earth: his sun
　　Hath need of you; and, if he takes
　　Last year's spoiled roses and remakes
Red summer with them, shall he shun
To steal your soft hearts every one,
　　O men and women, to enrich
His fair new transitory reign?

Are ye mere flowers to love again
　　With each fresh summer, knowing not which
Hath had the ripest of your bloom? —
Nay, but, for you, there is a doom
　　For ever making in the fair
Unalterable world above
The blue, unknown to your new love,
Irrevocable in your own
　　Sweet word: — O women, have a care
　　What if two come to claim your hair
Of God? — what if two shall have thrown
　　Their strong arms round your body, quite
　　Belonging with an equal right
To each for ever?

　　　　　　Would the place,
That bore so long the lovely grace
　　And wayward grief of Sarrazine,
Had never lost the tender spell
Of the half death that seemed to dwell
　　Out of time there on what was green
Of leaf and what was grey, on bird
And sleepless wraith; — would none had stirr'd

83

The gloomy magic making there
Some lone eternity to scare
Untoward striving fates and save
Her soul and body in one grave
    Of safe sleep unresponsive.
                            Yea,
For, at the last, I cannot say
What thing fell on her, when my lay
    Hath told you of this Chaitivel,
    Whom his fate made to love her well
And seek her, knowing nought of those
    That held her on the other side
    Of death. May this man's woe abide
With God for ever, among woes
    Some heaven of his — some mystic kiss
    Of Mary sweet shall turn to bliss!

It may be, still, for many a year
Sarrazine counted tear on tear
    To soften death unto the dead;
And many a thing, that they might hear
    Sometimes all faintly in the bed
    Of earth and leaves about them, said
— To touch them, if she might, and set
Some late desire of her at fret
    Within them — And, if, day or night,
    The grave had let them, fair and white,
And far more wondrous as she was
    Than in their memory, she would quite
    Have hailed that one who should have earned
To come to her in any pause
    Of death, with words that long had burned
    Her breast, and love that had long turned
To fair earth near their hearts. But now,
The graves grew winterly, and how
    It fared with them in that long sleep
She knew not: and they lay and dreamed,

Each one his dream, that he should keep
And hold her his for evermore.

Then Love, who rules the bright world, deemed
  That, all too well indeed, she bore
Such sorrow for the dead who seemed
  No longer worth one's caring for;
And, so, I ween, he sent one day
  This Chaitivel — who was a man
Most goodly, full of all the gay
  And thrilling summer-time that ran
Once more with rapture through the earth.

Alas, for her who gave him birth,
  And put indeed, upon his face
  And form, somewhat of her own grace
To make men love him, and her smile
Like magic in his mouth! No guile
  Was in her; and she saw him fair
And stayed with him, maybe a while,
  For the mere joy to see his hair
Grown lovely with youth's golden crown,
  And to behold his perfect bloom,
As of a flower that she had sown:
And, having loved indeed and known
  His heart, she left him to the doom
Another woman's love should make: —
  Alas, for her down in the tomb!

Was there no little deadly snake
Curled on the threshold, for her sake,
  To save him with its fiery fang?
Nay, but he entered; and this sad
Too lovely Sarrazine, all clad
  In clinging robes, with voice that sang
The piteous music of lone thought
  Most luringly, is unto him,
  As 'twere some fatal serpent, slim

And gracious that hath softly caught
  His soul twining about it close,
  Sinking it into ways of woes
Past saving.
               But his coming brought
The new strange miracle of love
  Upon her; and her heart, estranged
From all that once had seemed enough,
Sprang sudden at him as a bird
  Breaking a snare, or as a free
Blithe butterfly some second birth
  Lifts in the air, no more to be
The joyless worm it was on earth.

And, lo — once, when the night was sore,
And the world, for a faint space, bore
  The bitter nearness of its dead
Unwontedly, and every pore
  Of the chill graves seemed free to shed
  The white and ghastly dews long bred
In lone laborious agonies
Of those on whom the death-sleep lies
  Uneasily, — she said or sang,
  Mourning one last while, words that rang
With their full farewell in the ear
Of those her listening lovers, — clear
  With poignant doom of anguish, straight
  Awakening them to fight with fate
For ever.
          "Wheresoe'er ye be,
  Forgetting or remembering me,"
She sang, — "I bid you now farewell:
  Surely, I think, you shall not tell
  Hard things of me in heaven or hell:
  I pray God, that the grave be sweet
  About you, — yea, and, if ye keep
  Some sort of love of me through sleep, —

May the worms cease not to repeat
My sweet words lest ye wake and weep:
Only, if before God we meet,
I pray you, lovers, that no more
Ye tell me of the things I swore;
I loved you: may all death be sweet,
And peace be with you evermore.

"O lover, who had all delight
In winning me, — 'tis many a night,
Since, through the sweet hours lovingly,
I lay by you and you by me;
And now, perchance, if you should see
My flowerless beauty, loved by you,
Wasted to white and kissed all through
With sorrow, — scarcely might I seem
Your love of lost days or your dream
Down there in charmed sleep; and, to-day,
Why need I take your dream away?
— Sleep on; and think of me, I say,
Whatever sweet thing lets you lie
Content with death; I have made rich
Your grave indeed with tear and sigh;
And many a night hath been, through which
I prayed to God that I might die
And go down softly to you. Dear,
I do believe you would not hear;
You would not know or feel me near;
And, though I kissed you, till you saw
My wan face, I should never draw
One warm kiss from your lips, or thaw
The hard ice at your heart! What song
Of mine hath ever reached you? Long
Mad nights I lay awake, and wrought
My sorrowing heart to such a plaint
Of lone imploring words, I thought
Some of them surely must have brought

87

Your soul quite to me, roused with faint
Most piteous murmurings that made way
Through earth and leaves to where you lay.
And, if indeed death had not set
Some cold and very mighty spell
Upon you, making you forget
My face, yea, and your love, to dwell
With some unearthly dream, or rest
Dreamless and joyless in his breast
For ever,—O you had not failed
To steal up somehow, wearying night,
Death, dreams, and mystic ways of sight
And sound, till one fair path availed
To make you known to me. And now,
It seems we both who made the vow
Of love have fallen on either side
Somewhat away; and I, who chide
Thee never for it, hold, maybe,
At length the greater memory.

" 'Tis as though both of us had died
I think; and that lone grave of thine
Is scarce a harder place to pine
And gnaw the inmost heart and shed
Unsolaced tears in, than this bed,
Lonely and waste and white, where grief
Hath held me buried, years wrought sore
With sorrowing. No fair hope made brief
The agony it was, no more
To see one loved face bring relief
Of love: the hollow darkness bore
No dream to comfort; and the sight
Of the yet fair unruined white
Of my forlorn lost beauty pained
My spirit, showing me but chained
To so much more of death. Farewell:
Memory or sleep shall hold their spell

Unchanged upon you, till the name
Or thought of Sarrazine shall dwell
No more with you; and though, at last,
She winneth any sweet the past
Knew nothing of, she will not cast
The tenderness of many a day
Quickly and utterly away:
And, though quite other she became,
Surely the grave will feel the same."

But he who, living, had possest
  Her peerless body — who, till then,
  Rapt in sweet thought, had never known
How death grew chill and cold earth prest
  And walled him in, nor felt the stone
  Lie heavy between him and men, —
But he who, giving his soul's best
  Of heaven and God's eternal good,
Had won that woman to be his
  And change not: in mere solitude
Of death he woke, without a kiss,
And knew that fate was false; — the hiss
  Of a fell serpent seemed to bring
The words that woke him to his ear,
  Bitter with endless echoing,
And one long agony stretched clear
Out to his soul's eternity.
  Then, in the hollow of the tomb,
  Where his speech thundered into doom,
He answered her:

        "Woman," said he,
"Why have you been so false with me?
  Was it the waste thought of a day
I gave to you? — was it to win
  A wanton hour, I cast away
  My untried heavens and slew straightway

My greater unknown self within?
Was it to shrivel, with the sin
   Of mere rich revelling to dull
   My fallen soul once beautiful
Because of love, sharing the hell
Of harlots, that I chose to sell
   Usurious fate so much of vast,
Yea boundless, that lay known between
   Me and God only? So, at last,
   Not half way into doom, I find
This fails me, — this that should have been
   All heaven, this love that was to blind
So richly, I should ne'er have seen
The depth I dwelt in nor the height
   I forfeited; now, all behind,
   At once I see as many kings
As golden seeming days, with light
And lustre fading on them; bright
   Imperial crowns and goodly things
Fall from them hastily; they sit
   Dishonoured spectres of me, bare
In the bare past, abhorring it.
   If I could go back and repair
   One hour, one moment, to make fair
Eternity, — O I should seem
Not quite denuded of some dream
   To keep my soul unshamed before
The fiends and angels: but, indeed,
   I am too distant from that shore
Of life already; and no seed
   Is left for sowing any more.
Henceforth, a weed among much weed
Of foundered love and life, my soul
   Shall drift upon dark waves and waste
Upon the ceaseless seas that roll
   Through the lone Infinite.
                      Ah, haste

To live thy false life through, that I
May have that wrecked thing I did buy
　—A body for a soul!—for mine
I think you shall be, since I hold
A vow for every hair of gold,
　And destinies and all divine
Unalterable things of old
Witnessed your pale frail body bound
　To me immutably.—Ah, white
And worthless blossom, for delight
Of the lips only: Ah, the round
　Quite faultless fashioning of slim
　And sinuous side and shapely limb:
Ah, the delirious abyss
Of the mouth fainting in a kiss:—
Ah, all this, yea, though merely this,—
　Can make a goodly hell for him
Who loses heaven. And I grow sick
　Of waiting since I am no more
　Than one to kiss your bosom sore
For ever. Wherefore now the thick
　Polluted darkness? Wherefore gloom
And lonely wakings in the tomb?
Sin all, and, as you are, come quick
　And share my sin down here. How long
　Have I endured to dream among
The worms in faithful wretchedness—
　Sure you would come and lie along
Beside me and be sweet no less
Than I believed you? You would bless
　Some fond way for it all, and set
　Your mouth upon my mouth and let
The dreamed-of heaven begin: and, quite
　So noble was I with my faith,—
But for these sad words, I felt bite
The ground through to me—O I might
　Have ceased not trusting the sweet wraith

91

Of word and kiss and memory,
Of what I left you, endlessly!
    Here, in my place among the things
That change not, I myself, in all,
A changeless spirit past recall,
    With life's supreme rememberings
Unshaken in me,—here I feel
    And shudder at your shameful word.
    O woman, think you no fates heard,
When, passionately, beyond repeal,
You bade them know you mine and seal
    Your life and death so? See the blue—
    The sight you have up there with you
Most near to heaven,—and, if you can,
    Believe there is a God to let
    You change the word you would forget,
And quite revoke the doom a man
    Hath lived and died in! Change; and yet
You cannot change, but earth and sky
And death will keep you mine: and I—
Do not I live for ever?"

And it befell, another day,
When earth, well ravished of the gay
    Turbulent summer, fell to swoon
    Under the perfume of the moon,—
That Sarrazine, now rich at heart
With love's fond thinking, felt a part
    Of tender pity that must go
And find the grave out there beyond
    So many a sea, where, lone and low,
Beneath the palms, that Pharamond
    Lay buried, with his love of her,
    And bound as though he might not stir,
In meshes of soft growing gold.
And him, believing death must hold

So rigorously his heart and hands
That no fair singing in those lands
Had ever soothed him, — now she named;
And, murmuring softly of him, framed
    Her last thought of him in a song;
Singing it idly to the birds,
    And finding as she went along
Mere wanton music in the words:

Hath any loved you well, down there,
    Summer or winter through?
Down there, have you found any fair
    Laid in the grave with you?
Is death's long kiss a richer kiss
    Than mine was wont to be —
Or have you gone to some far bliss
    And quite forgotten me?

What soft enamouring of sleep
    Hath you in some soft way?
What charmed death holdeth you with deep
    Strange lure by night and day?
— A little space below the grass,
    Out of the sun and shade;
But worlds away from me, alas,
    Down there where you are laid?

My bright hair's waved and wasted gold,
    What is it now to thee —
Whether the rose-red life I hold
    Or white death holdeth me?
Down there you love the grave's own green,
    And evermore you rave
Of some sweet seraph you have seen
    Or dreamt of in the grave.

There you shall lie as you have lain,
    Though in the world above,

93

Another live your life again,
  Loving again your love:
Is it not sweet beneath the palm?
  Is not the warm day rife
With some long mystic golden calm
  Better than love and life?

The broad quaint odorous leaves like hands
  Weaving the fair day through,
Weave sleep no burnished bird withstands,
  While death weaves sleep for you;
And many a strange rich breathing sound
  Ravishes morn and noon:
And in that place you must have found
  Death a delicious swoon.

Hold me no longer for a word
  I used to say or sing:
Ah, long ago you must have heard
  So many a sweeter thing:
For rich earth must have reached your heart
  And turned the faith to flowers;
And warm wind stolen, part by part,
  Your soul through faithless hours.

And many a soft seed must have won
  Soil of some yielding thought,
To bring a bloom up to the sun
  That else had ne'er been brought;
And, doubtless, many a passionate hue
  Hath made that place more fair,
Making some passionate part of you
  Faithless to me down there.

But Pharamond heard that sweet sound,
  As the one strange thing waited for
  Through death; and, waking at the sore
Inconstant words, his hands unwound

94

The shining chain and tress that bound
　His limbs; and, in the glorious gloom
　Of that unconsecrated tomb,
He rose up, dumb and mighty, — pale
And terrible in blood-stained mail,
　And the gold on him as a belt, —
　He rose up, — a great soul that felt
Death ended ere a word from God:
And, going forth, he once more trod
　The waste ways of the human earth;
　And, terrible, and giving birth
To wide dismay, he crossed all lands,
Mountains and forests, and the sands
　Of deserts, and the pathless seas,
　And where suns burnt or snows did freeze
The summer, — going back to take
Her soul for vows she could not break.

And yet again, the last rich eve
　— Ere, for this Chaitivel, whom woe
Lay waiting for, she thought to leave
　The past for ever, yea, and go
　Through earths and heavens that ne'er should know
Other than her new love of her, —
Fearing not that the dead should stir
　Nor fate remember, — as they stayed,
Having used up their words and sighed
　To soften hours that yet delayed
Their souls from mingling to divide
　No more for ever, — Sarrazine,
Making her voice sad as might be
Some bird's last singing in the tree
　It nested in, said:

　　　　　　　"As I lean
This way upon your bosom, love,
Dreaming how it shall be above,

—Yea, when we go from star to star,
Finding innumerable ways
  To heaven,—a little thought flies far
Behind me, to the piteous days
Of one whom no soft memory stays,
  Maybe, from cursing me down there
  To death—who might have made life fair
And death less bitter, with one care,
One fond angelic word: O you,
  Whose love quite governs me and finds
  No will in me but your will binds
And turns it all to serving you—
You might have hated, if you knew
  How I was sterner than the death
  That gave him ease of the last breath,
Watching him hollow out his grave
  In his deep boyish love of me!
I had a thousand ways to save
  And strengthen him and make him flee;
  Nay, but I rather chose to see
His passionate face from day to day
  Consuming near me, knowing well
The different thoughts that made their prey
His heart, having a word to say
  —A word unsaid yet!—ah, what spell
Of peace should I delight to weave
  Over his grave there! I would take
The very waste the autumns leave
  Upon it, thinking, for his sake
Who lies there, no one stays to grieve,
  And I would change it into flowers
Forced up and fostered in my heart,
So I might soften the least part
  Of death, and make him quite forgive
And never hate me for the hours
  That made death sweeter than to live.

"Ah, love, but, now, I feel, as though
  I may forget all this and say
  It was another woman, yea,
And not this Sarrazine; for, so
Your love hath changed me, I may throw
   The past into a grave, and shrink
   From ever looking o'er the brink
To see the dead in it and see
A mouldering form of one like me."

And he who never had a joy
  In life because of her, — he heard
Quite plainly; and she did destroy
His slender hope with every word.
And, in the silence, his soul prayed
   That she might never take away
   The little joy it was to stay
Not far off in the place she made
Her heaven, to steal there unbetrayed,
And only see her from some shade.
But that night, ere they bade farewell,
A fear of unknown sadness fell
   Between them; and her lover went
To wait for joy, with such a heart
   As if an omen had been sent
Sorrow would come to take joy's part.

And when he sought her the next morn,
Lo, there was one who sat forlorn
  In the room with her, — a mute, pale,
Uncertain semblance of a man
Dreary and wasted past the span
  Of mortal sorrow; with a frail
Still passionate look he haunted her,
As though his pain changed with each stir
  Her hand or body made; — and, lo,
When, fearful, with a voice that burned
  His heart, he asked concerning him,

And why he came to her, — she turned
  And trembled, looking to and fro,
  And said, indeed, it was not so;
  Only a chill mist seemed to dim
Her sight; but surely none was there
  Beside himself and her. Then, straight
That other answered him from where
  He stood: a voice lent by mere fate
It seemed to be, and, thin as air,
  The void form seemed to vacillate,
As though sound shook it through and through:
  — "O lover, loved of her whom I
Must love unloved for ever, — you
Have naught to hate me for; e'en death
  Found little he might purify,
  When he divided the last sigh
I gave her with an earthly breath;
  And now I have long learnt to take
  Content in ways that could not break
Your peace or hers: none hindreth
  My soul from loving of her still:
  I pray God keep her from the chill
Of seeing me; and only this —
Which he hath granted for my bliss
  Shall all suffice me — to traverse
  Quite after her his universe
And dwell in the enchanted place
Her shadow filleth with her grace:
  Do thou not grudge me this I pray;
  And this she cannot take away."

The phantom flickered as a flame
  Blown blue and rent about by wind;
It seemed that every word became
A second agony like death
  Racking a soul caught and confined
  In the strained film of some last breath;

But, when the utterance ceased, the same —
  A cheerless wraith of form and face
  Shrinking into the room's far place
Of shade — that semblance did abide
  Before the living man who held
That living woman for his bride:
And still when, stricken with amaze,
He said: "That other hath his gaze
  Upon thee and but now he held
The speech thou must have heard," she grew
As one whom many deaths pursue,
  Pale and affrighted, but averred
  She nothing saw neither had heard
At all one speaking.
              And, behold,
As they sat speechless through the day
The spirit of the boy did stay
  Saddening them both and making cold
Their hearts; he stirred not from the gloom
Of the far corner of the room,
Crouched like a phantom in a tomb.

But a more fearful thing befell
Ere night; and they have done full well
To call this man the Chaitivel —
  The wretched one.
             For when, at eve,
  He went to her, and did believe
God and her love for evermore
Had power to make her his, — before
  He could have taken her or laid
A trembling hand on her, — there past
One between her and him. A blast
  Brought him in fearfully and made
  Unearthly winter chill the place;
A torn grave garment seemed the last

Earth-relic on him; form and face
Were mysteries where no man could trace
A part of former man, — within,
Without, he was become what sin
His soul invented; for, intense,
 He bore the hell of it. And this
 Was he who thought to buy the bliss
 Of holding one frail woman his
For ever, yea, at the expense
And loss of half his soul. Mere flame
 His thought seemed as he stood between,
 Finding a voice that might have been
A man's: and then in God's great name,
 He said: — "Touch not her body, thou!
 Mine only hath it been; and now
 I come and hold her for her vow
Mine only!"
     Then he took her, fair
 And deathly, fainting in the clutch
Of his grim darkness, with her hair
Sweeping the ground, and all her bare
 Delicious beauty free from touch
Borne desolately. Her lover there
Could find no way to strive at all
 With that appalling shape of dim
 Illimitable darkness: — him
No sword reached; but the blow did fall
 On Sarrazine: then, with a yell
 Unearthly, which no tongue could tell
The horror of, that spectre fled
Bearing the body of her dead,
 Dragging it inward to his hell
For ever.

   But her soul did stay:
Amazed with knowledge, and aghast
 To see, that moment and too late,

The real eternities and vast
  Terrific truths of love and fate.
The Wretched one sank down, and lay
  Knowing and suffering no more,
  As though he struck some dark closed door
At the blank end of being and ceased
  Against the darkness.— Who can say
  If one may die so, rent away
From life and after-life, and eased
  At once from destiny? How long
He felt not: but he felt again
The irremediable pain
  Recall him; and he woke among
Dread repetitions of the plain
And reeking horror: then his sight
  Met all things uttering the vast
  Relentless record: then, at last,
Beheld her soul remaining white
And whole and beautiful, no blight
  Or ruin cleaving on it. Free
  Of the torn frame now would she be,
And all acquitted! And the drear
And clanging night subsided near
  And far; and holy stillness grew.

  There, after all, remained they two
Together: death's mere subtle change
Dividing. And a new voice—strange,
  Ineffable in the night,— it seemed
One in a distant star were heard
Singing celestially,— brought word
  Revealing more than he had dreamed
Of love about him: for the speech
  Of her rapt spirit gazing straight
  Into the veilless face of fate
Was heard there; seeming to beseech

Unyielding destinies and strive
  With angels. Only, visible there,
In the clear wonder death did give
The face of her unfading soul,
  She seemed an angel, thrice more fair
Than she had seemed a woman.

                          Yea;
But now, for many a league away,
Where he was wandering by day
  And night, through many a land beyond
  The seas and deserts, — Pharamond
Beheld her in that hour: and, whole
Immeasurable miles between,
Across the dark, her soul had seen
  And trembled at him. Strong and loud
And dreadful were his feet that trod
  Thundering on mountain or on cloud —
Traversing earth and sea and air —
With vehement will defying God
To take her; for the golden hair
  Gleamed like a flaunted robe of flame
  Through earth and hell and heaven. He came
With no help of the wind or storm,
  Or miracle by sea or land,
Or deathly terror: in the form
  Of one most mighty, with the brand
Of blood upon stained steel he bore
  Till doom, and blood upon his hand,
And burning badge of one who swore
To bear his love for evermore,
  He came on through the night. And hate
  A long way off did emanate
And fly before him, making felt
  The coming of a fiend. And, lo,
Vengeful, a great way off, he dealt
  Defiance with his voice.

I know
This only: that, as one might go
Against one's death, the Chaitivel
Went against Pharamond that night
And met him; and the two did fight
Out on the moor.
And some can tell
How, while they fought and neither fell,
The fiend did mock the man and said:
"How long wilt thou contend with me,
A day, a year, a century?—
That thou art come to me arrayed
In this frail garb of flesh and blood,
And with these arms, as man to strive
For some dull perishable good
With man; or, thinkest thou to drive
Back to the grave this soul of mine
That brake the grave asunder? Yea,
Look on my soul and think if thine
May fight for an eternal thing
With me eternal?"
And they say
That, wrestling with the fiend, the man
Replied: "O Pharamond, I can;
And we must go on combating,
My soul and thy soul to the end!"

Then Pharamond's red sword did rend
The swart air; and they saw him smite
The man; and, ere the man was dead,
Once more a great voice shook the night
Saying: "Come up and let us fight
Unto the end, as thou hast said;
And peradventure, thou or I
May vanquish some day in the sky;
Or after ages have been spent,
Fighting through every element;

Or in the place where shadows dwell;
In thy far heaven or my far hell;
Or never; till some final gloom
Shall end all things and God entomb
Eternity!" . . .

And so they two fight on till doom.

Printed in Great Britain
by Amazon